MICHAI

THE ROARING TWENTIES

HOMOSEXUAL HEYDAY

Cover: Joseph Christian Leyendecker's Spring

© 2019

My books include: *Cellini* [a fully-revised 2018 edition], *Caravaggio* [a fully-revised 2018 edition], *Cesare Borgia, Renaissance Murders, TROY, Greek Homosexuality, ARGO, Alcibiades the Schoolboy, RENT BOYS, Buckingham, Homoerotic Art (in full color), Sailors and Homosexuality, The Essence of Being Gay, John (Jack) Nicholson, THE SACRED BAND, German Homosexuality, Gay Genius, SPARTA, Charles XII of Sweden, Mediterranean Homosexual Pleasure, CAPRI, Boarding School Homosexuality, American Homosexual Giants, HUSTLERS, Omnisexuality, the Death of Gay and Straight Sex* and *Christ has his John, I have my George: The History of British Homosexuality*. I live in the South of France.

DEDICATION

This book is dedicated to Sigmund Freud who wrote, in answer to a letter from a woman who feared for her son: ''I gather from your letter that your son is a homosexual. I am most impressed by the fact that you do not mention this term yourself in your information about him. May I question you why you avoid it? Homosexuality is nothing to be ashamed of, no vice, no degradation; it cannot be classified as an illness; we consider it to be a variation of the sexual function. Many highly respectable individuals of ancient and modern times have been homosexuals, several of the greatest men among them, Plato, Michelangelo, Leonardo da Vinci, etc. It is a great injustice to persecute homosexuality as a crime--and a cruelty, too. What analysis can do for your son runs in a different line. If he is unhappy, neurotic, torn by conflicts, inhibited in his social life, analysis may bring him harmony, peace of mind, full efficiency, whether he remains homosexual or not."

CONTENTS

PART ONE
Introduction
Page 6

PART TWO
Roaring Twenties England
Page 23
Prep Schools and Universities
Page 23
Cleveland Street Telegram Scandal
Page 35
The Order of Chaeronea
Page 38
Forster and Carpenter
Page 43

Somerset Maugham
Page 50
Lord Mountbatten and Prince Edward
Page 55
Noël Coward
Page 57
George Norman Douglas
Page 61

PART THREE
The Roaring Twenties' Apogee: Berlin
Page 63
Freud and William Reich
Page 73
Magnus Hirschfeld
Page 78
Sascha Schneider
Page 82
John Henry Mackay
Page 84
Max Liebermann
Page 85
Glyn Philpot
Page 85
Adolf Brand
Page 86
Wilhelm von Gloeden
Page 89
Friedrich Radszuweit
Page 91
Henry Gerber
Page 93
Thomas Mann

Page 94
The Wandervogel Movement
Page 97
Hans Blüher
Page 99
Arno Breker
Page 100

PART FOUR
The Belle Époque
Page 101
Cocteau
Page 114
André Gide
Page 140
Maurice Ravel
Page 153
Jacques d'Adelswärd-Fersen
Page 158

PART FIVE
The Roaring Twenties Made in America
Hollywood
Page 167
Griffith Park
Page 175
The Greystone Mansion
Page 176
Hearst
Page 177
The Scandal that Shocked the Roaring Twenties
Page 180
The Kiss

Page 183
The Garden of Allah
Page 185
Rudolph Valentino
Page 189
Ramón Novarro
Page 195
Bonnie and Clyde
Page 199
JC
[Joseph Christian Leyendecker]
Page 205

SOURCES
Page 206

INDEX
Page 214

≈≈≈≈≈≈≈≈≈≈≈≈≈≈≈≈≈≈≈≈≈≈≈≈≈≈≈≈≈≈≈≈≈

PART ONE

INTRODUCTION

The world has seen periods of wonders so great that they have eclipsed our own 21st Century: the immergence of Egypt, Athens under Pericles and Rome ruled by Augustus, da Vinci's Renaissance and, on the cusp of our own times, a period of intense sexual revival and creativity known as the Roaring Twenties, when theaters and cinemas were palaces that venerated the likes of Valentino and Garbo, undreamed of speed in the forms of automobiles and airplanes, speakeasies where flappers gained the foothold that would eventually give women the vote, industry that brought workers unheard-of prosperity and the homeowner laborsaving appliances, instant communication through the telephone and nightly entertainment by way of the radio. Skirts got shorter, women smoked in public, illegal champagne was swilled in quantity and cocaine made its appearance. Gigantic sports arenas shot up and the first sports heroes worshipped, cigarettes were shared on-screen between men and women during scenes of the most daring sensuality, languid looks across cabaret tables while listening to jazz, the corruption of the word jasm, meaning spirit, energy and vigor, itself derived from jism: spunk/semen, ground zero of all life, the embodiment of the Roaring Twenties.

Amusingly, women's liberation came in the form of women's desire to look boyish. They cut their hair short and chin length [bobbed], dresses were ''slinkish'', deemphasizing the size of buttocks and breasts, a sash or belt worn at hip level, and like boys they became flirtatious, a recklessness fueled by alcohol. Cosmetics, once reserved for prostitutes, became ''in'', as were bare legs and bare arms, the end product the Roaring Twenties flapper [the etymology of which is disputed]. Swim suits that had shown little more than ankle became far briefer, increasingly filmed by Hollywood directors who discovered that the more skin they showed, the bigger the box-office success. Thanks to the war, women entered the workforce, becoming less dependent on men, economic freedom that led to sexual freedom [succeeding so well in their liberation that today girls in dormitories chalk up the number of boys they've had, as boys have always kept track of their conquests]. During the time that concerns us, when boys lost their cherries around age 19, sex was basically ''petting'', during which boys tried to encourage girls to jerk them harder and faster, and girls tried to manoeuver so that a lad's fingers would find the right spot, not daring to tell him what she wanted, the whole certainly more erotic than today's no-nonsense fucking.

The reigning queen was Coco Chanel whose power attracted the likes of Stravinsky, as well as a legion of toy-boys that made Dawn, the sister of the Sun, blush a deep red when she got an early-morning glimpse of Chanel's goings-on. As Truman Capote said about one of his swans, if she'd had, on the exterior, all the dicks she'd had inside, she'd have resembled a porcupine.

Men wore suits, white shirts and the obligatory tie, their testosterone levels having already freed them sexually since the early cave dwellers. They had no need of cosmetics, and when their natural good-looks waned with age, their financial power automatically kicked in to assure a warming presence in their beds, heterosexual in the boondocks, predominantly male-male in Hollywood, pre-W.W. II Berlin (17), Paris (14) and London upper classes (10), upper classes that wore striped and herringbone suits, accompanied by straw boater hats in summer and dinner parties in tuxedos: raven-black vests, jackets, trousers and studs, unequaled in displaying the full extent of male beauty.

A tuxedo/dinner jacket by Leyendecker.

Berlin made wondrous advances in lighting and sanitation, becoming the cleanest and best lit city in the world, its post-W.W. I cafés and cabarets cracking with war survivors out to celebrate their being alive, a new anything-goes mentality encouraged by the knowledge that life was short, precarious and the end nigh, a city so apart that no other capital on the planet dared compete with Berlin's sexual experimentation, men dressing as women, women as men, where soldiers could double their pay by stepping out of their barracks and opening their flies for men who came the world over for what they could buy for a few pfennigs, the young and healthy soldiers making up for the low price paid by their ability to share their semen several times a day and still have enough for girlfriends and wives. Berlin was also the world center of studies on homosexuality, extensively covered in Part Three.

In Paris, too, the nights were jammed with men

who filled the streets, from the Moulin Rouge to the Boeuf sur le Toit, men who indulged in women, caviar and absinthe, a just return for the rigors of the war, the deadly reminder of which is found on monuments at the entrance of every village in France, endless lists of those who sacrificed their lives so that champagne could again flow, while Dawn blushed at the view of sleeping lovers, sprawled out on beds, naked, after a night of Roaring Twenties lubricity.

In Paris the Roaring Twenties was known as the Belle Époque, and so aware were men and women of the tenuousness of existence that a new philosophy was spawn, existentialism, the perfect justification for their search of pleasure at all costs.

Only in England was their no name for the period, a land left behind by the economic wonders that followed the war, drab years for the masses, while for men with means there were never more brothels, and in no other land on earth were there more shared orgasms than in English prep schools and universities (4). The outside world filtered through thanks to wireless radios that brought news and entertainment into living rooms [the BBC founded in 1922], and consummation gained a tenuous foothold, thanks to enterprises like Marks and Spencer. The first cars were bought, and new housing made such an upsurge that every village in England today has homes that date from the '20s. The economic downturn was intensified by a combination of bad government and America's surge in inventions and production, an explosion that remained unrivaled until threatened by post-W.W. II Japan and today's China. Where British salaries should have increased exponentially to the loss of labor

10

decimated by the war, competition with the United States and Europe saw the price of coal plunge, with its accompanying decrease in pay, leading to the General Strike of 1926, when three million workers ceased production. Britain depended on selling coal, cotton, steel and iron, middle-ages technology in comparison to the cars, new tissues and chemicals that were making their appearance in the U.S., a disadvantage that culminated in the Great Depression of 1930. The boom in sales in the States, backed by mass production and buying on credit, produced a bubble in which even taxis drivers became millionaires, on paper, while the United Kingdom knew only deflation and stagnation. To pay off the war debt, and forestall bankruptcy, Britain chose fiscal austerity and high interest rates that stifled investment and spending, industry unable to borrow in order to expand, a downward spiral that led to layoffs.

The dichotomy was that England had at its fingertips the greatest economist of the period, Maynard Keynes. Keynes warned that the Sterling was overvalued compared to the dollar, which made the price of English goods 20% more expensive than those in America, fiscal suicide that Keynes, still largely unknown, was unable to redress. Keynes was an end product of a British prep-school and university education, a man of such brilliance that at this very moment, somewhere in the world, economists and philosophers have the name of John Maynard Keynes on their lips, perhaps furiously in favor of his ideas, perhaps furiously against, but all are as respectful as before an ancient god. It was Keynes who was the first to spearhead, in the 1930s, the then-revolutionary idea of free markets. Keynes fought for virile intervention in fiscal and monetary policies, thanks to which the disaster of 1929 came to an end, as well as the world financial crises of 2007-2008.

In 1990 TIME magazine wrote, ''his radical idea that governments should spend money they don't have may have saved capitalism.''

Keynes made the cover of TIME on the 31st of December 1965. TIME wrote, ''We are all Keynesians now.''

Keynes was born in Cambridge, Cambridgeshire, to upper-middle-class parents, his father an economist and lecturer at Cambridge, his mother a social reformer, the perfect storm in the creation of this humanist genius. His brother became a surgeon, his sister married a Nobel Prize-winning physiologist. Lovingly raised, all three children never strayed far from home and the care of both parents. Keynes was damned with poor health but compensated with brilliance in mathematics, the classics and history, which saw him into Eton with a scholarship. In 1902 Keynes went to King's College, Cambridge, thanks to another scholarship, this one in mathematics, even though the true love of his life was philosophy and

history. He was an active member of the Apostles (21), as well as one of the original members of the Bloomsbury Set (16). His family love instilled an eternal optimism in Keynes, self-confidence and the belief that man could do good and that governments could and must come to the aid of its citizens. He began publishing his first articles on economics in 1909, at age 26, and in 1911 became editor of *The Economic Journal*. He accepted a government position in the Treasury in 1915 and gave lectures. At Versailles, at the end of the First World War, he fought to prevent the allies' demands for German compensation that he knew would destroy the German people, a fight he lost, which led, first, to his resignation from the Treasury and, second, W.W. II.

In 1919 he became chairman of the British Bank of Northern Commerce in exchange for working one morning per week, at a salary of £2,000, £95,000 today. Keynes wrote that the purpose of work was to provide leisure, and felt that everyone should work fewer hours and have longer vacations.

At the height of the Great Depression he wrote *The Means to Prosperity*, based on the need for government public spending, a copy of which went to Franklin Roosevelt, and Keynesian became the adjective applied to all new economic ideas. Without government intervention to increase expenditures, insisted Keynes, low employment would continue. His contribution to W.W. II came in his 1940 book *How to Pay for the War*. Keynes was given a seat as one of the directors of the Bank of England, as well as a hereditary peerage that came with another seat, this one in the House of Lords. At Bretton Woods Keynes argued for a world currency, the bancor, and a world central bank, ideas overruled by Americans, although the International Monetary Fund was established as a compromise.

Keynes was circumcised, the reason being the Masturbation Panic: The panic stemmed from the beliefs of certain doctors, most notably one whose name has come down to us, Simon-André Tissot, 1728-1797, who claimed that the loss of an ounce of semen equaled the loss of forty ounces of blood, a crippling factor that could lead to the loss of eyesight, to diseases and, due to increased blood flow to the brain, insanity, consequences as damning as religious threats of Hell due to the nefarious, unnatural act of self-pollution, the mortal enemy of procreation. In the mid-1850s masturbation was blamed for the corruption of morals, as well as vile thoughts that threatened the salvation of the soul itself, accompanied by the exhaustion of the entire nervous system. Boys were ordered to do physical exercises until they dropped from fatigue, to take cold showers, and fathers were advised to tie up their sons' hands at night [presumably behind their backs, although the most exquisite sensations could then be enjoyed by gently rubbing oneself against one's mattress, as the reader well knows]. Some surgeons recommended replacing the testicles of masturbators with healthy ones [which led to castration because the new testicles were rejected by the body, and death if the surgery was done in unclean surroundings, often the case in those times]. Freud showed interest in the possibilities of the operation--for others, not himself.

The foreskin and its movement up and down the glans was blamed for drawing a boy's attention to his penis, leading to masturbation and the mental and physical illnesses that followed. Keynes went under the knife at age 8, an incredibly painful procedure, the agony lasting for weeks. Some doctors at the time suggested the operation be done without anesthetics, as the boy would then identify the pain as a punishment for touching the penis. When Keynes was 11 his father had the pockets of his overcoat sewn up so he couldn't fondle himself [his father confided to his diary], and most probably those of his trousers too. Richard Davenport-Hines, in his *The Seven Lives of John Maynard Keynes,* states that a politician, Lord Hailsham, still remembered the pain of his circumcision 70 years later, the blood ''and my sense of betrayal by the adult world.'' [W.H. Auden was circumcised at age 7, after which he became erotically captivated by boys who had foreskins, as was the pornography star Al Parker (13), an obsession extensively discussed in my book *Phallus*.]

Keynes's obsession with numbers pushed him to note even his sexual adventures. From May 1908 to February 1909, he wrote in his diary, he had 61 intimate encounters, mainly with Duncan Grant and with both Strachey brothers, Lytton and James (16). From February 1909 to February 1910 he had 65 encounters; 26 from February 1910 to February 1911, and 39 from February 1911 to February 1912. His diaries were heavily encoded but the following items have been deciphered: He wrote of having sex with ''a 16-year-old under Etna'' and ''the liftboy of Vauxhall''. In 1911 he had 16 C's, 4 A's and 5 W's. Encoders guess the A's were ass-contacts, the C's cocksucking and the W's wanks [jerking off] with boys/men. Baths and saunas were the easiest places to find contacts, and Keynes knew all the parks, hotels and sites where guardsmen earned extra cash. As sodomy was punishable by imprisonment, under the same law that had seen Oscar Wilde sent away, guardsmen had to be careful. When one of Keynes's favorites was found out and was dismissed from service, he took cyanide, such suicides being, apparently, *far* from exceptional. The 2008 edition of *The Atlantic* stated that Keynes's compulsion to calculate everything began in childhood, when he counted and remembered the number of steps leading up to the houses on the street where he lived, as well as detailed records of his expenses and his golf scores. In his diaries he gave the initials of the men he was bedding, GLS for Lytton Strachey, DG for Grant and nicknames, Tressider for the King's college Provost J.T. Sheppard. What went on within the Bloomsbury Set was described by Keynes's biographer Robert Skidelsky as a ''sexual merry-to-round.'' At the time, claimed his friends, he was as obsessed with whom he would share an orgasm as he was later with economic affairs or philosophy. Keynes wrote this about the Bloomsbury Set, ''We repudiated general rules. We repudiated customary morals, conventions and traditional wisdom. We were, in the strict sense of the term, immoralists.'' For Keynes self-denial was bad, self-indulgence good [which was the undercurrent of his financial policy too]. ''After all,'' he wrote, ''in the long run we're all dead.''

    At Keynes's passing, in 1946, he was worth £500,000 [£20 million today], and he possessed the works of Picasso, Degas, Cézanne, Modigliani, Braque and Seurat. He died of a heart attack at age 62.

[For far more, see my book *The Bloomsbury Set*.]

In the boondocks of all of these countries the masses continued to labor, dependent on priests for baptisms, marriages and burials, priests often as ignorant as they, but priests who promised them eternal life. Most knew nothing of sexual attraction towards other men, even those who frequented rivers to watch boys bathe naked, and who inundated their bellies at night, the remembrance of the lads firing their breathless self-pleasuring (28), most certain, absolutely certain, that in the whole world only they harbored such despicable urges.

All great periods in history were preceded by times of horrid darkness, the Renaissance by the Middle Ages, the Roaring Twenties by W.W. I, the death of millions creating a dearth of labor that saw full employment and salaries skyrocket [with the exception of England]. Less cited, but far, far deadlier, was the influenza pandemic from 1918 to 1919 that added 70 million more dead, far greater than the 40 million who had fallen during the Great War.

American economic motivation after W.W.I was the opposite of W.W. II's generous Marshall Plan. Post-W.W.I tariffs made foreign imports so expensive that American production was favored, the twin benefits of mass production and buying on credit were goosed by American inventions and the advent of mass publicity, in itself a source of employment for thousands. [Americans were the first to bring together publicity and affliction, churning out products that covered everything from acid in digestion to athletes' foot, body odor, underarm offense, bad breath--inventing the scary Latin word halitosis along the way, some products, like Listerine, still on sale a hundred years after their discovery.] Industry was given government subsidies, a Keynesian incentive for renewal and expansion, aided by limitless power from coal, dams and newly discovered oil, as well as raw materials in abundance, making America self-sufficient. Prices spiraled *downward*, a car that sold for $850 in 1908 cost $290 in 1925. Assembly lines churned out goods that could be purchased over a period of months, even years, an innovation-mentality that dared try anything new, a population both ambitious and optimistic from birth, where opportunity knew no limit and a boy was convinced he could start out sweeping the floors of a bank and end up its president. A mindset that existed nowhere else on the planet.

    The most beautiful boys and girls, those that won beauty contests in high schools and fueled the wet dreams of their adolescent schoolmates, took trains out West, their imaginations fired by the stories of waitresses who became the stars of the new film studios, mass arrivals that saw Los Angeles's population exploded to 4 million in the early 1900s, trains that, due to competition of two rival railways, saw costs lowered to $1 a head for the journey. The film industry changed the mores of the period, showing everything from how to dress to how to light a lady's cigarette, and on-screen sensuality enhanced the belief that each male had the right to a girl of his own [while backstage in Hollywood actors and producers were too busy fucking the daily trainloads of beauties to bother remembering their names].

The discovery of vast supplies of oil made a barrel cheaper than an equivalent barrel of water, and American farms, seemingly endless, produced ever-cheaper food, nourishing a generation of boys that would outstrip their European counterparts by a good four inches in height.

Hollywood came to every American, and increasingly to every European, in theaters and cinemas that were, in the great capitals, cathedral in size, providing audiences, in America, with cartoons and b-rated films that preceded the marquee main attraction, a paradise, cool in America's broiling summers, heated in devastating winters. By the end of the Roaring Twenties 100 million cinema tickets were being sold *each week*.

In America the wealth was shared by all through increased wages [Ford offered $5 a day in 1914, causing a stamped on his factories, and later allowed workers to put in 8 hours daily instead of the usual 9]. Anyone could buy shares in American companies, and because everyone was doing so, shares exploded in value, making America a nation of millionaires--until, of course, the burst of the bubble that ended the Roaring Twenties.

Gangsters came into vogue in 1920 with the ratification of the 18th Amendment that banned the drinking of alcohol. The money from illicit booze and hundreds of speakeasies went into thousands of gangster pockets, a percentage of which found its way to politicians and police officers. Al Capone was known by all and admired by many, the founder of the later mafia. Similar debacles took root in other countries, like the communist seizure of power in China in 1921, the creation of the USSR in 1922, and Mussolini's march on Rome, also in 1922.

Britain's troubles continued with the partition of Ireland, a poisonous situation in the news even today, 2019. The BBC charged its listeners £10, [£550 today], a tax that added to Britain's sinking economy, a draining of buying power that could have been avoided by permitting publicity, which would have boosted the sale of British consumer goods. English men and women found some relief by losing themselves in a book by Agatha Christie, whose disappearance for 11 days caused an unprecedented manhunt and the subject of books written about her ever since, headlines she shared with Carter's discovery of the tomb of Tutankhamun. Carter's perseverance was surpassed by Alexander Flemings discovery of penicillin, saving the lives of hundreds of millions, while Britain's John Baird developed television's first transmitter.

In Chicago, American consumerism got a shot in the arm by the opening of Sears Roebuck in 1925, bankrupt in 2018, proof that Amazon's founder Jeff Bezos was perhaps right in maintaining that even today's Amazon would have a limited lifespan. In 1925 the first motel opened in California and in 1926 the construction of Route 66 filled the new motels with those going West, as well as the mushrooming phenomenon known as tourism. Route 66 remained America's coast-to-coast roadway until Eisenhower discovered Germany's autobahns after the war, the origin of today's highways. The Scopes Monkey Trial made the headlines in 1925, Scopes found guilty of teaching evolution and fined $100 [$1,500 today], money he didn't have to pay, thanks to a technicality. Lindbergh flew from New York to Paris in 1927, a man who was justifiably impressed by Hitler who had saved Germany from economic devastation, before bringing on its apocalypse. Other Lindbergh-level heroes received the first blows of the chisel at Mount Rushmore, although Babe Ruth, and his homerun record that stood for 70 years, wasn't among them. Walt Disney created Mickey Mouse, decades prior to his having a sexual threesome with director George Cukor and actor James Dean (32), and cross-dressing homosexual J. Edgar Hoover was put in charge of the Bureau of Investigation [in 1924]. American Robert Goddard fired off the first liquid-fueled rocket in 1926, good or bad news, depending on the reader's convictions. Car radios came into existence in 1929, and that year the Academy Awards made its debut.

Historically, religious influence, both Catholic and Protestant, labeled sex as a necessary, if unpleasant, obligation in the production of children, and many girls probably did go to their wedding night bed in complete ignorance of what awaited them. Little restraint was expected from men, but women were looked up to as the guardians of virtue and morality. The Comstock laws of 1873 forbade the distribution and even the discussion of contraceptives through the mail. Venereal diseases reached epidemic levels during W.W.I, which led to sex education and the distribution of the ''male sheath'', although current research tends to prove that the vast percentage of venereal diseases was contracted prior to a soldier's entrance into the service and *not* in the brothels of Europe, leading one to believe that lots more was going on, sexually, in the States than previously imagined. Thanks to the use of condoms and an increased understanding of ovulation, the birthrate decreased during the 1920s, from 3.5 per couple to 2.3. Adolescent petting was of course unthinkable in homes, which accounted for part of the success of the back rows in cinemas, helped along by Hollywood movies which showed boys, on giant screens, that kissing involved also necks and ears, while girls saw the felicity that love could bring, thanks to erotic scenes like those between Garbo and John Gilbert in *Queen Christina*, manna for boys because girls permitted them to go still farther. And when cinemas couldn't provide the cover for what girls were increasingly willing to surrender, increasingly affordable cars proved themselves exciting bedrooms on four wheels, the reality of which encouraged carmakers to install more extensive backseats.

Literature too was becoming more daring, the books of D.H. Lawrence instant bestsellers. Divorce, common in Hollywood where it was central to the sale of magazines, had an impact on the public in general, freeing thousands from their oath of ''until death do us part.'' Hollywood invented the pool party, a soft-core version of which made its way into suburbia, although slow dances during which a boy's admiration for his date was nudged against her thigh rarely led to full intercourse, whereas in well-educated and well-heeled families sex was common, as was the exchange of partners, as portrayed in Larry McMurtry's semi-autobiographical *The Last Picture Show*. The actual intercourse normally took place in bedrooms, while in

Hollywood poolside fucking in mass orgies became the ultimate in eroticism. Boys began to accept the fact that they would perhaps not marry a virgin, a requirement that had endured from the Ancient Greeks and Romans to the Renaissance, the justification for male-male sexual release [due to the Brinks-like protection of girls].

And finally, in Chicago Henry Gerber founded his Society for Human Rights, fully covered in Part Three due to Gerber's German roots.

PART TWO

Roaring Twenties England

Homosexuality in England had at its basis two roots: British prep schools and the Oscar Wilde trial of 1895. Perp-school sexuality took place in dormitories, veritable sanctuaries where in some schools the boys were locked in for the night, a playing field where boys gave free rein to the urges of their budding puberty, allowing them, after years of trial and error among themselves, to pinpoint the true nature of their desires, heterosexual, homosexual or omnisexual, an occasion of discovery unique in Europe. Not only were the boys free to explore every facet of the testosterone-fueled urges that governed their nights as well as part of their days, when holes in their pockets gave access to friends with whom they could find relief in any library stack or corridor niche, in addition their professors, fired red-hot by the knowledge of what was going on, roused their lubricity further by introducing texts in Greek and Latin that idealized the love between males, all in the hope that the lads would allow, at the very least, mutual caresses to orgasm during the private tutorials on the semen stained couches in the professors' chambers.

Prep schools and universities, as sanctuarized as churches, were homosexual safe havens that separated the elite from the heathen masses, those who prosecuted save-sex misbehavior since Henry VIII established the death penalty in 1533, replaced only in 1861 by imprisonment, for which Wilde received two years, a trial that shook the foundations of English society because Wilde had been part of the untouchable English elite, and because his theatrical popularity had made him the age's Shakespeare. [Wilde's full life can be found in my book *Christ Has His John, I Have My George*: *The History of British Homosexuality*.]

The Spawning Grounds of English Homosexuality: Its Prep Schools and Universities

Because Roaring Twenties' sexuality in Britain had its roots in prep schools and universities, a brief history of both is needed here.

Oxford and Cambridge are referred to together as Oxbridge, schools for the rich and aristocratic where the dons, following a Middle-Ages custom, were not married, but where an inexhaustible supply of highborn boys were at their disposal. Lads were trained academically and homosexually on courses of Greek and Latin classics, the first step of which were the prep schools of Repton, Harrow, Winchester and others. Of disputed educational value in the past, today

Oxbridge rank in the top 5 of the world's universities, and many of the schools that prepare students for entrance into Oxbridge are often, intellectually, *today*, the *crème de la crème*.

Oxbridge were ruled by dons, professors who lived in the upper-class world they created in their image, exclusive, privileged to an unbelievable extend because they could do as they pleased with university monies, live in lavish surroundings, kowtowed to like emperors by teachers and staff.

Margaret Thatcher ended their paradise in the 1980s by asking the question What-the-hell-are-they-doing with Britain's money?, and, when she found out, she put a stop to it.

Cambridge was founded in 1209 by scholars fleeing Oxford because of disputes between the great Henry II's far-less-great son King John and Pope Innocent III, as to who should appoint the Archbishop of Canterbury. In 1231 both Oxford and Cambridge received charters from Henry III which freed them from paying taxes, as well as the right, accorded by Pope Gregory IX, for graduates to teach wherever they wished.

During the Middle Ages grammar, rhetoric, logic, mathematics, geometry and astrology were taught, augmented with mind-liberating Humanities during the Renaissance. Six new colleges were added to Cambridge between 1430 and 1496, for a total of 31 today. With the Reformation Henry VIII named Cambridge don Thomas Cranmar as the first Protestant Archbishop of Canterbury, who was soon afterwards beheaded by the Catholic Queen Mary. The Cambridge teacher William Tyndale translated the

Bible into English, and because the Bible was exclusively the church's domain, he was burned at the stake.

Cambridge men were among the Pilgrims that founded America and Cambridge graduate John Harvard endowed the university that adopted his name. Cambridge Oliver Cromwell saw to the beheading of Charles I.

Isaac Newton was a Fellow of Trinity College who didn't believe in the religious Trinity but was personally supported by Charles II who left him free to discover his laws of motion and gravity, in addition to calculus, and tell men that although God set all in motion, He had other things to do than the day-to-day running of the universe, thereby freeing men's minds to look into the subject themselves.

Cambridge man Francis Bacon was making progress in science while giving his lover Buckingham advice as to how to manipulate *his* lover James I/VI (2). The Cambridge atheist Halley was discovering his comet, while people began to talk about the Cambridge student Charles Darwin--and have never stopped.

The Enlightenment at an end, women were allowed into Oxford in 1869 and into Cambridge in 1920, although without full rights until 1947. The likes of the Bloomsbury Set set the pace afterwards (16).

The Society of Apostles was formed at Cambridge in 1820 where homosexually physical friendships were formed, called Lower Sodomy, or what was called Higher Sodomy, non-sexual male bonding (21). Society members created, later, the Bloomsbury Set.

Schools were homosexual settings in the 1800s where the highborn went to do boys, where learning was far less important than playing both musical beds and sports, the athletic heroes of which were chosen to be Fag Masters and had their pick of the prettiest lads, employing them to bring them off manually or lying on their stomachs, and whose influence was reinforced by handing the lads, post-orgasm, to their friends for their personal gratification. Among themselves, in their own dormitories, the young boys continued their inexhaustible sexual hijinks which John Symonds called ruthless orgies.

In tandem with the mediocrity of an education in both Oxford and Cambridge, was the poor physical condition of the writers, poets and other aesthetes, of the 1800s and early 1900s, that frequented both schools. Yet they were convinced of their excellence, even if many were nothing but arrogant wimps, often moneyed, who paid for rent-boys in pre-W.W. II Germany and Italy, an easy task in those years where a lad would sell himself for the proverbial Hersey Bar [after the war most boys sold themselves for even less because they were *starving*] (23). Many Oxbridge boys didn't see war because they were physically unfit to be induced, poor eyesight, bird-breasted chests, precocious varicose-veins, girlish biceps. The exceptions were spectacular: Rupert Brooke, Byron and several others, yet even Byron was only attractive when illness brought his weight down to human levels. Few of the men from Oxford and Cambridge resembled the boys seen in gymnasiums or on the wrestling mats, while the boys they paid for were often physically splendid. Proud of the clothes they donned for extravagant meals and the robes they wore in the inner chambers of their rooms, coquettish and swishy, they wouldn't have turned on even a girl, let alone far more demanding males. The writer Wyndham Lewis called Bloomsbury Set's Duncan Grant ''a little fairy-like individual who would have received no attention in any country except England.'' In a nutshell, that's exactly what I'm talking about. Which is why the English themselves often look to other lands for good sex.

Tutors and students took sherry together and shared meals, after which what naturally happened when young men wished to please their masters did happen, consisting most probably of little more than mutual masturbation, but when it took place one time it was hard to see how the inexperienced student could [or would dare to] ward off a second and then a third occasion, and so on, which meant, in the end, that it was a disgraceful debasement of what should have been a striving towards academic excellence. It was putrid exploitation, exploitation that George Mallory may have had to agree to under his tutor Arthur Benson, as will be seen. In the Greek way the lover served as a tutor, whose quest was to instruct the boy as well as sexually share acts of love, but the difference was that the boy always chose the man, and that the man was but a few years older, handsome thanks to boys being physically trained, from childhood, to care for their bodies, whereas in Cambridge and Oxford the tutors were flabby, pale-skinned, often androgynous wrecks. We know nothing of Byron's sexual encounters with his tutors, although they most certainly took place, but we do know he had the consolation of lads younger than he, for whom his experience, eloquence, fine clothes, wealth, title and tastes made him a god, a god who willingly released them from their virginity if they had managed to keep it till then, which, knowing boarding schools that catered to lads 12 and over, was highly improbable.

About his own schooling, John Addington Symonds wrote: ''The talk in the dormitories and studies was of the grossest character, with repulsive scenes of onanism, mutual masturbation and obscene orgies of naked boys in bed together. There was no refinement, just animal lust.'' The first order that Makepeace Thackeray received on his first day at school from a schoolmate was ''Come & frig me,'' he wrote later.

How much the men who left both universities, to become truly great warriors and administrators, owed to Oxford and Cambridge training cannot of course be known, but there were many who thought that bonding through the exchange of sexual favors was destined to ready the graduates for their role as builders and leaders of the British Empire, an inane belief but one supported, in a way, by Plato who had Aristophanes put this in one of his plays: ''While they are boys they love men and like to lie with them and embrace them, and these are the best of the boys and youths. The evidence is that it's these boys, when they grow up, who become the best men in politics.''

Many of these aristocratic pansies were in no way comparable to the admirable *men* who died at Thermopylae (18) and in the ranks of the Sacred Band of Thebes (19), nor those who fought in the Crimea and Gallipoli, who ruled the seas for generations and made the second most populous country in the world, India, a democracy, who were decimated in the First World

War and saved England from disaster in the Second, and most assuredly had nothing to do with the homosexual trio of fops, Blunt, Burgess and Maclean, who betrayed their country to the murderous Soviets.

The first English school was thought to have been establish in 598 A.D., the purpose of which was to produce those who ran the church, and as the members were priests they were also celibate, a tradition that continued later on, encompassing the first university dons. The nobility was educated in Latin in which the Bible was written, although the curriculum was extended to rhetoric, mathematics, astronomy and music, exactly the same classes taught in ancient Rome, which were carbon copies of those in earlier Greece. As pure, unbroken voices were necessary for church services, boys from every horizon were recruited, especially among the poor, boys who were offered the rudiments of an education, free of charge, boys who filled the countless ranks of those sexually used by the celibates who ran the schools. Convinced in one way or another that they were accomplishing part of God's will, little convincing was necessary to have them bend over. Later thousands of men became priests thanks to the infinite pool of boys that made up the church, from the very first schools right up to today's, religious institutions where, for some recondite reason, the church can keep clericals out of prison simply by paying damages. For the boys, historically, this was nonetheless their ticket out of poverty, many becoming church clericals and boy abusers in their own time.

While nobles were taught at home by private tutors, the poor were welcomed into schools like Eton that Henry VIII set up in 1442 to provide pre-pubescent lads for his choirs. Dozens of schools were founded by Henry and Elizabeth on the ashes of those destroyed in order for the Anglican church to reign supreme.

Because schools were far between, boys eventually became boarders in towns around the schools. This was easily accepted because the nobles had farmed out their boys to be educated in the houses of other nobles for years, at around age 7. Eventually it was realized that these fee-paying lads could become a huge source of profit if they were housed in schools. This helped too for disciplinary reasons as the closer the boys were physically to their tutors, the easier it was to control them. Thus the advent of boarding schools. Soon an incredible *esprit de corps* formed between the boys, meaning that a boy interviewed for a job by someone who had been to his college was nearly certain to be hired. And it was not uncommon that boys dying in war had a last thought for their college house before that of their God. When the tenderness of first love is mingled with all the other first experiences of life, an inherent part of youth, no armed concrete is more solid.

The early schools were based on Latin and scriptures, Greek and the classics came later, during the Renaissance. And although England was making incredible strides in exploration, discovery, rule over other lands, advances in medicine under Harvey and science under Newton, public schools continued on as arrogant social functions aimed at showing off one's eccentricities in fine clothing, to honor the best in food and wines, and to have free, unsuppressed and unlimited sexual access to new boys entering each year. Nothing the world has known could compete with the wild orgiastic no-holds-barred sex in the entirely unsupervised dormitories. Moreover, boys slept two to a bed in the first boarding schools, until 1805 at Harrow. No wonder men would later die with the burning memory of youthful lust alive in their breasts like incandescent coals, and why men, become fathers, tolerated nearly every excess in their sons, an exclusively British phenomenon, and the reason that once a Brit ended his school years he exiled himself for extended and numerous visits to more liberal skies, especially those of Italy and pre-W.W. II Germany, while in Britain homosexuality was punished by death until 1835, when the last man was beheaded.

As there were few masters in the early schools to control hundreds of lads, beatings were among the most appalling to have existed, and they and other forms of abuse have continued right up to the present as the reader will soon see. Floggings by headmasters inspired cruelty among the boys, and even Bertrand Russell wrote that the big boys hit him so he hit the little boys, ''that's fair'', he concluded.

Dormitories were no more than male brothels. To make sex easy and accessible, [a healthy boy being able to ejaculate six times daily], the linings of their pockets were cut away so they could play with themselves, even in class, and two boys could especially practice mutual masturbation, withdrawing their hands from the other's pocket in a second if interrupted. For unknown reasons homosexuality was more fashionable in some schools than others, and even in schools where it was fashionable it suddenly ceased being so, whereas where it was little practiced it might come back with a bang. In one school a headmaster who succeeded in rounding up a huge number of boys, said to have been around 100, and having them all beaten for some forgotten rascality, was applauded by the boys afterwards for having been clever enough to catch them all.

It would seem that the earlier boys start having sex among themselves, the easier sex is throughout their lives. On the other hand, boys who enter into sexual relations with girls later on are more stressful and fearful, and the sexual satisfaction is far less to what they had known with other boys at puberty. The result is unhappy marriages and divorce. Sex is easy between boys because they are simply clones of each other; there is little that is unfamiliar for them to discover; they've known from puberty what turns them on.

The holidays in those early schools were short, 20 to 30 days a year from 1500 to 1700, while the academic part of the day was short, 4 hours at Eton in the 1750s, half-days on Thursdays and on Saturdays, and no schooling at all Tuesdays and Sundays.

The age was brutal--the 1600s and 1700s--when sailors were lashed to death, parents were cruel to their children, children could be imprisoned for stealing a handkerchief, poor houses where children were beaten and exposed to every form of sexual vice, several children to a bed, and where headmasters were told explicitly by parents to birch them at their first obstinacy. It was a time when children were farmed out to wet nurses until around age 7 when, if they hadn't died of a childhood disease as at least half did, they were packed off to boarding schools. An example: like Byron, Talleyrand had had a clubfoot and had been sent to poor provincials to be brought up without the slightest education. Miraculously, a relative discovered him and took him to Paris to the rich residence of his parents where he and the boy walked in on a party of wigged noblemen, Talleyrand in filthy rags, bringing an immediate end to the chamber music and festivities. ''This is your son!'' the relative bellowed to the amazed parents.

Abuse in schools could go on unhampered because the headmasters washed their hands at what went on between the lads, especially as they knew they couldn't control it, and because they had their own lives to lead. The fact that boys were in class for so few hours gave them acres of free time, and nowhere was the saying idle hands are the devil's workshop more true. Their parents bought their own freedom by dispatching the boys to schools, giving them enough money to buy the drink and food and whores they coveted, rampaging through the streets, free to wreak havoc because the towns people could not complain to headmasters who would do nothing, nor the boys' parents who were most often their betters and who resided far away. *And* the money jingling in the lads' pockets would eventually find its way into town shops.

Education in these schools was wholly secondary to the comfort and prestige of the place parents parked their children. Such academic dinosaurs would have disappeared eons ago had it not been for the fact that they evolved, and thanks to their wealth are now able to hire the best teachers who give the best education, and today rank among the world's top institutions. In public schools the sanction is immediate: when a school drops in rank its rich subscribers turn elsewhere, while *state* schools go on and on, no matter how mediocre the instruction. Luckily for America its universities are so wealthy the students are admitted through exams, meaning that the poorest church mouse can become a veritable pillar of society, even if the vast majority of the students are prepared by the best American prep schools, something out of the reach of all but the most dedicated, hard-working poor. Yet the tradition of starting off cleaning school toilets and ending up the school dean [in America, of course] still [I hope] prevails, an impossibility in Europe.

The attitude today, sexually, is that boys can do what they want as long as they are discreet and there is no sexual exploitation, a form of don't ask/don't tell. And that's the way it should be. Boys should be left alone, in the sense that adults must be excluded because they can force boys by their positions [priests and headmasters], their sweet talk [as men are infinitely more experienced and knowledgeable than boys], money and other forms of pressure and coercion. The rule of older boys poses a conundrum because young lads can be drawn to their prowess, especially when they're successful athletes. Older boys can show responsibility in the Greek way, become a teacher and protector, encouraging the boy to greater heights. In that case, who can rightfully cast the first stone?

[The full history of sexual discovery in prep schools and universities can be found in my book *Boarding School Homosexuality*.]

The Cleveland Street Telegram Scandal

Pre-Roaring Twenties scandals were intimately responsible for the immense differences between how sex took place during the period London, Paris and Berlin. In 1889 a scandal of huge porportions broke out, the Cleveland Street Telegram Scandal: There was a sudden increase in the number of telegrams sent between members of the aristocracy and upper classes. It eventually turned out that boys delivering them were highly amenable to exchanging sexual services for a few coins, which in a sense did no one any harm as boys are ever in need of finances to fulfill their desires, while their healthy young bodies can easily care for the sexual wishes of older men, without depleting the lads of their natural ability to ''spend'' nearly at will [with girls, for example, later on during the day or night, should they so wish].

But the boys were found out when the police were called in to investigate the theft of some money in a telegraph office. One of the boys working there, age 15, was searched and a personal fortune was found on him, 14 shillings, equivalent to several weeks' salary. Accused of stealing the sum from the telegraph office, the boy felt it was less damaging to tell the truth, that the money had come from gentlemen who made use of his young person.

Some of the lads.

He gave up the name of the boy, 18, who had recruited him, as well as friends who did the same as he, and added that for additional funds they all worked for a certain Charles Hammond who ran a male brothel on Cleveland Street, frequented, it was rumored, by the man who was next in line for the British throne, Prince Albert Victor, and his squire, Lord Arthur Somerset, who fled to Paris before he could be questioned.

A cartoon published at the time.

One of the telegraph boys warned Hammond who made an escape, avoiding a possible imprisonment of two years.

Through his squire Somerset, a lawyer was hired, Arthur Newton, who got the boys off with 4 to 9 months of hard labor. The lawyer got money to Hammond, allowing him to install himself in America. Somerset lived out the rest of his days in the south of France, dying in 1926.

The Order of Chaeronea

The Order of Chaeronea was founded in 1897 by George Cecil Ives, 1867-1950, who himself best described its aim: ''We believe in the glory of passion. We believe in the inspiration of emotion. We believe in the holiness of love.'' They also believed in homoeroticism, and although they went out of their way to deny that their Order was a means to meet like-minded and like-bodied mates, that's exactly what took place, as they knew it would. Oscar Wilde and his paramour Douglas were members, among a few cited below.

Ives stated that the Order was ascetic, but that some ''passionate sensuality'' may take place. In fact, this became the bases of the Order, as it was in the Cambridge Apostles (21), set up as a debating club but under Maynard Keynes and others evolved into a kind of licentious backroom for seducing boys, individually through persuasion or coercion, and through all-male dinners that ended in sexual free-for-alls. While tutors were using Greek texts to lure boys onto their semen-stained couches, the Order relied on Walt Whitman as their central showpiece, Whitman who claimed that all boys should prostitute themselves sometime during their lives, as a way of gaining life-experience and useful pocket change.

The Order of Chaeronea founder.

The Order was named after the defeat of the Sacred Band of Thebes, by Alexander the Great and his father Philip, in the year 338 B.C., from which date the order delineated time, as we do A.D., meaning that this year, 2019, is, by the Order's calculation, 2357.

As the story of the Sacred Band is unique in the hallowed history of love between men, I refer the reader to my book *The Sacred Band*, priced at the lowest cost permitted by the editors in order for it to be accessible to all.

Erected by Thebans in memory of the 300 lovers and belovèds that fell before Philip and his son Alexander the Great in 338 B.C., the Lion of Chaeronea was restored by British archeologist Cecil Harcourt Smith, thanks to funds from the Order of Chaeronea in 1902. Nearby are the cremated remains of Philip's Macedonian soldiers.

Of the principle members of the Order we know this:

Kains Jackson, 1857-1933, poet, lawyer and editor, was important in publicizing the paintings of Henry Scott Tuke, Tuke a hugely important figure in boy-eroticism. A prominent member of the Order, Jackson was also a close friend of Lord Douglas and J.A. Symonds.

Samuel Cottam, 1863-1943, poet and priest, was a member of the Order and lover of Edwin Bradford, likewise a poet and priest. Cottam published the openly gay *Chameleon*, a magazine used against Oscar Wilde during his trial because Wilde had contributed articles to it. Cottam and Bradford became chaplains at the

Anglican church of St. George in Paris, where they jointly seduced the choir boys, Bradford's biographer listing a score of lads he dedicated poems to, apparently in thanks for the pleasure they'd accorded him.

On the gravestone of Montague Summers (1880-1948) one reads an inscription he often repeated in life: ''Tell me strange things.'' And there were few as strange as Summers himself. His ambition was to become an Anglican priest, which he succeeded in doing, and then a Catholic priest when he converted, a title he apparently bestowed on himself, the prestige of both functions that he alternatively used to put himself in contact with the young boys he delighted in seducing, as this was the routine for priests, then as today, as despicable then as it is today.

Summers was interested in the occult and in witchcraft, writing *The History of Witchcraft and Demonology*, in which he describes witches as loathsomely obscene, perfectionists in poisoning, blackmail and crime, abortionists who encourage adultery in ladies and lewdness in gentlemen.

He believed in vampires, writing *The Vampire, His Kith and Kin* and *The Vampire in Europe*, and he proclaimed his certainty of the existence of werewolves with his *The Werewolf*. He dressed the part: black soutane, black cloak and black buckled shoes, a man *The Times* called ''A throwback to the Middle Ages.'' He was a member of the British Society for the Study of Sex Psychology, for which he wrote an article on the Marquis de Sade.

John Gambril Nicholson (1866-1931) taught English in a very large number of schools throughout England and Wales, and even coached a football team, manna from Heaven as he liked boys from age 12, one of whom he invokes in his autobiographical *Romance of a Choir-Boy*, and a thirteen-year-old, Ernest Mather, to whom he dedicated one of his collections of poems. Poem writing was the *raison d'être* of many homosexuals during the time, with a few, like Byron, making money from their *oeuvre*. He wrote, ''Physical intimacies are but surface emotions, forgotten as soon as they are satisfied; whereas spiritual intimacies live in the heart, they are part of our eternal life, and reach beyond the stars.'' Poppycock he vomited between bouts of ''physical intimacies''.

Nicholson with Alec Melling, another of his boys, the poor-quality image is the only one available.

Here is a list of Chaeronea aims, used to sanctify their real purpose, access to the content of as many adolescent boys' briefs as they could manage in a lifetime.
    1- To form a social and fraternal secret order for men who love men.

2- To encourage the cultivation of a homosexual, morally, ethically, culturally and spiritually.
3- To use Ancient Greece as a model, which includes lover/belovèd consensual, ethical and responsible sexual relations.
4- To aspire to the Greek body ideal [the case with Greek boys and their athletic older lovers, but certainly not Chaeronea men, pasty skinned, paunchy and gone to fat].
5- To form an army of lovers to fight against homophobia, to come to the aid of fellow gays, and to contribute to the betterment of one's community.
6- To cease mimicking Judeo-Christian ideals. [On this my personal view is that despite incalculable gains in knowledge, we still refuse to stand on our own two feet, putting our faith in ourselves rather than superstitious nonsense, fine in times when men had no understanding of disease and death, and needed the encouragement and compassion of an unseen Being bigger than ourselves, beliefs that nonetheless saw, among the Aztecs, perhaps a million hearts of a million lads cut from their young chests and held up, still throbbing, to the Sun, in the hope that it would rise again the following day.]

Forster and Carpenter

E.M. Forster and Edward Carpenter were two major writers during the Roaring Twenties in Britain. E.M. Forster, 1879-1970, was above all a Roaring Twenties' humanist, acknowledged as such when named President of Cambridge Humanists and a member of the British Humanist Association until his death at age 81. A great aunt left him £800,000 in today's money, which freed him from any form of servitude. He was an on-the-fringe member of the Bloomsbury Set (16), and a King's College, Cambridge, student. His name is associated with several men, among them Christopher Isherwood and Benjamin Britten.

His travels took him throughout Europe, especially Italy, which inspired two books, *Where Angels Fear to Tread* and *A Room with a View*. He was secretary to a maharaja and several visits to India inspired his most read book, the 1924 *A Passage to India*.

Among what is called his "loving relationships" was a very long one with a married policeman.

He was nominated for the Nobel Prize 13 times and he wrote his last book at age 35.

Forster

The problem with E.M. Forster's book *Maurice* was that it had a happy ending. Maurice meets a gamekeeper, they fall in love, decide to remain with each other throughout life, *and do so*. Had the book ended in the usual homosexual tragedy Forster might have decided to have it published, as then everyone could plainly see the consequences of immoral love.

The book begins with prep-school boarding-school love and goes on to university love [Greek texts encouraged by horny tutors], the whole apparently based on the true lives of Edward Carpenter, 1844-1929, and his lover George Merrill. It was finally published in 1971, a year after his death, 60 years after its creation.

Interestingly, Maurice tries to cure himself of his love of boys through hypnotism before deciding to be of service to the working class by running a boxing gym, the compensation being the naked lads under the showers.

A humanist like Forster, Edward Carpenter chose to aid the lower classes, as well as finding his sexual companions among them: ''the grimy and oil-besmeared figure of a stoker'' or ''the thick-thighed hot course-fleshed young bricklayer with a strap around his waist.'' He also doted on Parisian rent-boys.

He decried the industrial smog of Sheffield that was killing thousands and realized that only a strong socialist movement had the potential of putting things right.

Educated at Brighton College and Trinity Hall, Cambridge, at his father's death he inherited enough to become financially independent. He bought a farm that he worked, while writing his book of poems, *Towards Democracy*.

He met George Merrill, a working-class man without a formal education, in 1891 at age 47, and they lived together 27 years despite the hysteria due to the Oscar Wilde trial and the Criminal Law Bill that outlawed all forms of homosexual contact. Concerning Merrill he wrote, in his *Intermediate Sex*: "Eros is a great leveler. Perhaps the true Democracy rests, more firmly than anywhere else, on a sentiment which easily passes the bounds of class and caste, and unites in the closest affection the most estranged ranks of society. It is noticeable how often [homosexuals] of good position and breeding are drawn to rougher types, as of manual workers, and frequently very permanent alliances grow up in this way, which although not publicly acknowledged have a decided influence on social institutions, customs and political tendencies." The book was the foundation of the LGBT movement [lesbian, gay, bisexual and transgender].

Merrill and Carpenter.

Carpenter's last years were devoted to homosexual rights, as well as the protection of the environment and animals, the benefits of a vegetarian diet and the necessity of pacifism. George Orwell attacked him as representing ''every fruit-juice drinker, nudist, sandal wearer and sex maniac'' in the Socialist movement.

Merrill died in 1928, bringing on a stroke that kept Carpenter paralyzed until his own death in 1929.

Edward Carpenter did what he could when writing *The Intermediate Sex*, given the homophobia of the times, the existing laws, and fears that his friends would be open to calumny. The book is very thin and so the copy sent to me, a reprint, is in such huge type that it's difficult to read! Here are the salient parts:

Carpenter begins by saying that all women have a dash of men in them and vice-versa, which means that today both sexes are drawing nearer, both appreciating music, art and bicycling.

The intermediate sex is a man like any other, healthy, well-developed, muscular, with a powerful brain and a high standard of conduct [Carpenter is describing, of course, his conception of himself]. They do not necessarily force themselves to marry and have children, and if they do marry it is often platonically [as several Bloomsbury men did (16)].

Those who realize what they are have serious inner struggles, particularly because they share the emotional soul-nature of women, even though, he stresses again, they are every bit as masculine as other men in body and mind.

Men who take to them are lucky "as they walk on roses without ever having to fear the thorns [because the intermediates are so sweet] and there is no better nurse when one is ill."

Carpenter offers a list of exceptional intermediates, including Michelangelo, Shakespeare, Marlowe, Alexander the Great and Caesar.

He cites the Greeks, briefly mentioning Cleomachus who, when preparing to leave for war, was kissed by his beloved who tenderly placed Cleomachus' helmet on his head.

He invokes Melville [a homosexual] who spoke about the "extravagant" friendships between Polynesian males, and naturally Patrocles and Achilles (24), Alexander and Hephaestion (25) came up, as well as quoting a Persian poem, "Bitter and sweet is the parting kiss on the lips of a friend."

Plato comes in with a quote from the *Symposium*, "I know not any greater blessing to a young man beginning life than a virtuous lover, or to the lover than a beloved youth."

Carpenter goes on to say that many intermediates marry for "ethical" and "social consideration," and form friendships with females that nonetheless are "of no avail to overcome the distaste on the part of one to sexual intercourse."

He elliptically uses expressions such as "the love in which we are dealing," and nearly never the word homosexual.

Carpenter says this of school friendships: "...between the young thing and its teacher, its importance in the educational sense can hardly be overrated." A 16-year-old says this about his tutor: "I would have died for him ten times over. My plan to meet him [to come across him casually, as it were] was that of a lad for his sweetheart, and when I saw him my heart beat so violently that it caught my breath, and I could not speak. We met in ___, and for the weeks that he stayed there I thought of nothing else--thought of him night and day--and when he returned to London I used to write him weekly letters, veritable love-letters of many sheets in length."

"Anyone who has had experience of schoolboys knows well enough that they are capable of forming these romantic and devoted attachments," writes Carpenter.

Carpenter wrote that there was no sex education in British schools, and as a consequence a boy's desire for knowledge is filled in by his comrades: "Contraband information is smuggled in ... smut takes the place of decent explanations; unhealthy practices follow; the sacredness of sex goes its way, never to return." He states that "boys and youths must be trusted to form decent and loving friendships ... considerably more important than friendship." "Boys and youths" perpetuate the Greek ideal of boys always having older friends [lovers for the Greeks], the idea being that one instructs the other. "This was exactly the goldmine Byron fell upon. Because of his clubfoot he was mocked in college and his first year was a disaster. So the idea came, when he was in his second year, to show the new boys around and help them, warmly, to get to know the ropes. He never had a lonely night again," a quote from my book *Venice*, a part of which recounts Byron's life.

He wrote that "the capacity of a man to devote himself to the welfare of boys and youths ought not to go wasted." And later states: "That capacity for sincere affection which causes an elder man to care so deeply for the welfare of a youth or boy is met and responded to by a similar capacity in the young thing of devotion to an elder man. This fact is not always recognized; but I have known cases of boys and even young men who would feel the most romantic attachments to quite mature men, sometimes as much as forty or fifty years of age, and only for them." This is, naturally, every older man's wet dream. One wonders at Carpenter's naivety in thinking that the boy would love a much older man for himself rather than what he was in a position to do for the boy--although, who knows?, this may have taken place.

Somerset Maugham

The defining feature of Maugham's life, 1874-1965, was certainly the loss of his mother, at age 8, whom he adored and whose picture never left him throughout all his years on earth. His father died two years later and Maugham was farmed out to a cold uncle who put him in a boarding school where he was ridiculed for his small size and his inadequacy in English, as he had been born in Paris where his father was a legal expert at the British Embassy.

At 16 he went to Heidelberg University where he had his first sexual relations--outside of those mandatory in boarding schools--with John Ellingham Brooks, 26, a Cambridge graduate in law and a pianist who would later spend time with Maugham on Capri, starting 1895: ''I came for lunch and stayed for life.'' About Brooks Maugham wrote: ''He can discover nothing for himself. He intends to write but has neither the energy, imagination or will. He is weak, vain and profoundly selfish.'' [So much for love.] In Capri Brooks shared his digs with Edward Frederick Benson, 1867-1940, known as Fred, a novelist, archeologist and short story writer. Benson was an exceptional athlete, representing Britain in figure skating. Given the times, there were only the slightest allusions to homosexuality in Benson's writing. Of Benson's five brothers and sisters, all were "queer", as he himself put it, which was indeed the case.

Benson, the photo on the left taken at Eton by Baron Corvo [Corvo's life is recounted in my book *Venice*].

Maugham went on to study medicine and became a doctor, but the success of his first novel allowed him to devote all his time to writing, eventually making him the highest paid writer of the 1930s. But his time as a doctor had been vital: "I saw how men died. I saw how they bore pain. I saw what hope looked like, fear and relief." By age 40 he had written 10 plays and 10 novels. His lifelong lover was Gerald Haxton who remained with Maugham until his death, 30 years after their meeting.

Maugham traveled widely, writing the *Moon and Sixpence*, the life of Gauguin, and was a part of MI6 from which experience he wrote a series of short stories having for hero a sophisticated gentleman spy whom Fleming used for his James Bond. He lived the rest of his life at Cap Ferrat, the most exclusive and beautiful part of the French Riviera.

During his time with Haxton he had another lover, Alan Searle. He adopted the boy as his son, making the lad literally filthy rich at Maugham's death at age 91, [even if the adoption was later overturned to protect the interests of Maugham's daughter whose mother had married Maugham because she said he had made her pregnant, after which they divorced]. Maugham had also been deeply in love with Harry Philips, and so afraid were they of being exposed in an Oscar-Wilde-type scandal [Maugham had been 21 during Oscar's trial] that they only met in Paris for their sexual trysts. In 1919 Haxton was deported from Britain for being caught in a homosexual act. What happened was this: In November 1915 the military police, looking for deserters, burst into Haxton's hotel room and found him *in fragrante delicto* with a young man, John Lindsell. Haxton, an American born in San Francisco, was deported as an undesirable alien. The reason for the deportation has always been attributed to the hotel incident, but many historians are unsure. What is certain is that the Haxton dossier has been placed in a special ''100-year category'' and will therefore not be disclosed in my lifetime, at least.

Thereafter Haxton and Maugham met only during Maugham's travels, which were extremely frequent.

Haxton, and Haxton with Maugham [pictures of Philips and Searle are, alas, unavailable, and even these are atrocious].

Losing his mother, and school trauma, left Maugham extremely shy and caused a stutter. He said Haxton was indispensable to him in his writing because he was an extravert who interviewed the people Maugham shied away from. Haxton was said to have been obnoxious to Maugham, ordering him about, telling him to fetch his drinks [Haxton was an alcoholic] and ran up gambling debts that Maugham, wealthy, had no difficulty, nor hesitancy, covering. It was evident that Haxton was the *raison d'être* of Maugham's life, and friends claimed that Maugham's eyes would light up the moment Haxton entered the room. On the other hand, Maugham was reported to have treated Searle as badly as Haxton treated him, but Searle, described as rough trade (5), appreciated Maugham's collection of pornography and the pool parties Maugham threw. For although Maugham was repeatedly said to have been timid, his villa in France was *the* center for boys, obligatorily bathing naked in his pool, and the orgies that took place there rivaled those of Gloeden's at Taormina, with local French lads filling the place of Gloeden's Italians.

In 1905 Maugham was in Capri with his friend Harry Philips. They stayed at the Villa Valentino. Maugham wrote, ''Capri is charming and the people immoral.'' In 1905 the number of tourists to Capri was already 30,000, especially Germans.

A photo taken at Maugham's Riviera pool, amidst 9 acres of gardens, the boys catered to by 13 servants. Maugham was at times absent, in Switzerland, having injections of sheep fetus cells, supposedly to help him keep up with the lads.

In the heyday of story writing Maugham was paid $2,500 for each by Hearst magazines, and one story, ''Rain'', brought in $1 million in royalties, a fabulous sum for 1923 [worth, in fact, 14 million of today's dollars], when it was made into the film that launched the career of Joan Crawford. In all, 98 films were made from his material, just in his lifetime! Yet, about himself, Maugham was perhaps right: ''I know just where I stand: in the very front row of the second-rate.''

Lord Mountbatten (1900-1979) and Prince Edward (1894-1972)

This is what Gore Vidal had to say about Mountbatten (1900-1979) in his memoir *Palimpsest*: ''For a time Denham [a world-class rent-boy (23)] moved in the glamorous Mountbatten world, which was, contrary to what you may read in all the biographies, boldly bisexual. There was a whole group around Mountbatten--Paul of Yugoslavia, Paul of Greece and various others darting in and out. Mountbatten was a kind of master of the revels.'' A lifelong companion was Peter Murphy whom he had ''known'' since his Cambridge years and to whom he gave a yearly allowance of £600 until Murphy's death.

Mountbatten's title at birth was Seine Durchlaucht Prinz Ludwig von Battenberg, changed during W.W.I to Mountbatten, the savvy translation of Battenberg. The night before his assassination Caesar dined with Brutus, perhaps his son, soon to be his murderer. The subject of the table conversation was the perfect death, which Caesar wanted rapid and unexpected. Brutus granted his wish. At age 79 Mountbatten likewise was awarded a rapid exit when the IRA blew him and his boat to smithereens, bring an end to an incredibly fulfilled life, one normally found only in dreams. [The

IRA scum also ended the lives of two lads on the ship, aged 14 and 15.]

Here Mountbatten bathing with his purported lover Edward Prince of Wales [the future King Edward VIII] on H.M.S. *Renown* in 1920, amidst countless sailors, his for the choosing, who referred to him as Mountbottom, and not necessarily behind his back as he did little to hide his bisexuality, as well as having a sense of humor. He is said to have proclaimed, ''Edwina [his wife] and I spent all our married lives getting into other people's bed''. The felicity on his grinning face is stunning.

During W.W. II Mountbatten commanded the 5th Destroyer Flotilla, his ship, the *Kelly*, sunk by German aviation off the coast of Crete, about which Noël Coward, his lover, made the film *In Which We Serve*. Mountbatten planned commando raids, one of which, against Dieppe, was a disaster that cost thousands of casualties, and that Field Marshal Montgomery claimed was ill conceived from the start. From then on his initiatives were mostly quashed by Churchill. During the Potsdam Conference Stalin was so unimpressed by Mountbatten that he couldn't even get an invitation to visit the Soviet Union.

Mountbatten was named the last Viceroy of India in 1947 and was unable to keep Pakistan from separating from India, with the massacres that followed. He, his wife and Nehru were said to have formed a *ménage-à-trois,* as all three were bisexual.

He allegedly planned a coup against the government of Harold Wilson, backed by the army, with Mountbatten himself replacing Wilson. In 2009 MI5 published an official history *The Defense of the Realm* in which they confirmed the plot against Wilson, and that the participants were only a group of discontented officers.

Noël Coward
1899-1973

Coward, 1899-1973, was an incredible *touche-à-tout*: plays, screenplays, several volumes of short stories, a three-volume autobiography, poetry, and also served as chief of the British propaganda office in Paris and was a member of the Secret Service. He made his stage début at age 11 and was known for his wit and flamboyance, a man TIME magazine said had "cheek and chic, pose and poise." Encouraged by his mother, he tried out and was accepted as a child actor in numerous plays and already, at age 14, he became the lover of his protégé Philip Streatfeild.

Coward, 14, with Streatfeild, a painter.

At age 20 he appeared in his own play *I'll Leave it to You*. At age 25 he produced a play in America and took as lover stockbroker Jack Wilson. He wrote *Hayfever* at age 26, the best loved of his plays today, and the song "Mad about the Boy." By age 30 he was pulling in £50,000, £2,000,000 in today's money. During W.W. II he worked for the Secret Service to drum up war support in America, while in Britain, where the press knew nothing of his secret assignment, he was criticized for staying abroad. Churchill told him he could help out best by touring the troops, which he did in Europe, Africa and Asia, a kind of American-style Bob Hope, acting and singing.

In 1955 he took a cabaret act he himself mounted to Las Vegas, so successful that CBS hired him to direct t.v. specials. He wrote a score of plays and acted in films, even offered a role in *Dr. No* that he turned down saying, "No, no, no, a thousand times, no." Incredibly, he was offered the star role in *Lolita*, that he refused.

The love of his life was actor Graham Payn, with whom he remained until his death.

Graham Payn remained with Coward most of his life, Payn dying in their shared Swiss home in 2005 at age 85.

The number of his lovers was countless, one of whom was the composer Ned Rorem. He began an affair with the Duke of Kent when Coward was 24, that lasted 20 years until the Duke's death in a plane crash.

Both Rorem and the Duke were ravishing.

About himself he wrote: ''My sense of my importance to the world is relatively small. On the other hand, my sense of my importance to myself is tremendous." And when a TIME interviewer apologized for asking the questions that everyone else asked about him, he replied: "Not at all. I'm fascinated by the subject."

At age 60 he suffered a nervous breakdown when the heterosexual actor he was relentlessly chasing, William Traylor, tried to commit suicide due to Coward's stalking, a scandal Coward paid to keep away from the press. Once over the breakdown, he tried to arrange himself by having a complete facelift.

On the occasion of his 70th anniversary Lord Mountbatten, with whom Coward had been seriously entangled when young, said: "There are probably greater painters than Noël, greater novelists than Noël, greater librettists, greater composers of music, greater singers, greater dancers, greater comedians, greater tragedians, greater stage producers, greater film directors, greater cabaret artists, greater TV stars. If there are, they are fourteen different people. Only one man combined all fourteen different labels – The Master." In 1970, at age 71, he was knighted.

He may have been 71, but he never ceased using his wit and fame to seduce boys, often in their teens. One young man who finally surrendered [hounded like the boy who tried to commit suicide] was present when he kicked his secretary in the shin, bringing blood, a man [Coward] the boy described as being callous and cruel, his heart dead from years of alcoholism and megalomania, who thought he had earned the right to every boy on the planet. Cecil Beaton--the same age as Coward--noted that he had "become a fat old turtle with slits for eyes, no upper teeth, hunched, bent--the lot."

Coward before the shipwreck of old age.

One of his several homes on Jamaica was visited by Ian Fleming, Laurence Olivier, Sophia Loren, Elizabeth Taylor and Burton, Alec Guinness, Katherine Hepburn, Sean Connery, Peter O'Toole, et al. Handsome rent-boys were sent first-class air tickets to join him on the island, where they were sumptuously entertained. It was there he died at age 73.

George Norman Douglas
1868-1952

Douglas took his life in 1952 on Capri and the inscription he wanted on his tombstone, an ode by Horace, was: *omnes eodem cogimur, We are all driven to the same end.* And his final *living* words, before taking an overdose: ''Get those fucking nuns away from me!''

Douglas died a Caprese, as he had been made a citizen of the island (12), and was a close friend of Graham Greene. Born in Thüringen Austria, he was raised mostly in Scotland. Douglas did diplomatic service in St. Petersburg from whence he was expulsed for supposedly heterosexual activity involving well-connected Russian wives. The year before he wrote his best-known book, *South Wind* (1917), he jumped bail in London and fled to Italy, having been accused of an indecent assault on a 16-year-old boy, what Douglas said was an excessive punishment for ''giving him some cakes and a shilling.'' This charge was reinforced by another that came at the same time, an accusation of sexual offences [we don't know the details] against two brothers, aged 10 and 12. [At age 31 he had a sexual affair with the 15-year-old son of his mistress, and admitted to a friend, concerning his preference for young boys, ''I've always liked a small possession (small lads), attached to a very large possession (dicks).''] Douglas's friends Joseph Conrad and Compton Mackenzie counseled him to jump bail. [A word on Compton Mackenzie in passing. He too lived on Capri and wrote books with lesbian themes. One can only dream of a life like Compton Mackenzie's. Compton derives from the stage name his family adopted, Henry Compton, for example, a known Shakespearean actor. Among his hundred books is one on the Battle of Marathon, another on the Battle of Salamis, Greek subjects very close to my heart. His comic novel *Whisky Galore* spawned a film and t.v. series, and his *Sinister Street* influenced writers from George Orwell to Henry James. *Thin Ice* evokes the life of a homosexual politician and four of his books were on his years in British Intelligence. His autobiography consists of ten volumes and in 1952 he was knighted. There won't be a separate chapter on him because it's not at all certain that he was, to some extent, homosexual.]

   Douglas had married and his wife, in requesting custody of their children, accused him of pedophilia, consisting of the "rather faunesque pursuit of young boys," she testified.

Homosexual scandals in Italy obliged him to leave for the French Riviera before becoming a Caprese. John Sutherland wrote that his prose, before becoming outdated, made him "one of the smartest things going", a fashion that lasted "the whole of his long depraved life, one jump ahead of the law."

His book *Together* is a travel account of his summer in Austria just after W.W.I, with observations on rural life, descriptions of mountains and forests, pretty boring and uneventful, except for the fact that he made the trip with René, a 15-year-old Italian boy.

PART THREE

THE ROARING TWENTIES' APOGEE: BERLIN

The Weimar Republic replaced the German Empire in 1919, under which Berlin became the uncontested capital of Roaring Twenties' homosexuality. It was named Weimar after the city where it was constitutionally created, although its official name was the German Reich. It was a success in that it renegotiated the terms of the Treaty of Versailles so that Germany paid few of the war reparations demanded of it. Lubricity in Weimar was unbridled and omnisexual. It was homoerotic, ephebophile and sadomasochistic. Like Berlin today, and Sans Francisco, everything went, and a boy--a schoolboy--could earn a living as soon as he was old enough to understand what was going on around him. Soldiers rounded off their wages by fucking the likes of the writer Christopher Isherwood and the poet W.H. Auden. Boys could be butch [one of whom Auden hired to give him regular beatings]. Historian Louis Snyder claimed that Röhm believed homosexuals could outdo straights in brawls, killing ''and slaughtering for the hell of it.'' Historian Thomas Tuchs wrote that Hitler himself felt that homosexuals were second to none when it came to ''beating up anyone opposed to Nazis.''

What took place in Berlin preceded Paris, London and New York to such an extent that homosexuality was said to have originated there, at least since the Dark Ages of male-male sexuality that followed the Christianization of Ancient Rome.

What is amazing in the history of love among males was that after the Renaissance there followed an age darker than the Middle Ages which had preceded the Renaissance. Love between males during the Renaissance could be punished by death, but in reality under Lorenzo *Il Magnifico* de' Medici one got off easily because everyone was doing it (8), sharing, at some point in their lives, orgasms with other males. As girls were worth their weight in gold thanks to advantageous marriages that would enrich their husbands, they were kept locked away. Unlike a boy who could offer himself to a hundred passing hands or mouths or anuses and still claim innocence, a girl had one chance, after which the fruit was eternally spoiled.

After the Renaissance we stepped back into the dark, where lads, in the 1800s, could not comprehend their attraction to lads, those they had seen swimming in rivers and lakes, naked and so beautiful the boys dreaming of them inundated their own bellies in equally wondrous rivers and lakes. Till then, men were thought [by some] to have become homosexual because they were so insatiable sexually that they simply turned to men as an alternative to women who now bored them. Sexuality was malleable, and one could alter it at will. To keep boys on the right track laws were harsh, although thankfully the death penalty had been dropped, except, in one of life's never-ending paradoxes, in Berlin--until 1868. It was felt that men who cared for other men were in reality women trapped in a man's body, which would not only account for their searching out other men, but would account too for those who were effeminate. The woman within was seeking an outlet for her femininity.

Men who were lucky, mostly educated men who emigrated to Berlin, could find sexual satisfaction in the garrison city of 400,000 where soldiers padded their pay by selling themselves, and that for generations. The unlucky ones, the vast majority, may have felt that they and their sexuality were alone in the world, that no others shared their dreams and lust. These would live and die alone. Following the French Revolution, laws against sodomy were abolished [in 1791]. Under French influence they were abrogated also in Spain, Belgium, the Netherlands and Italy. Certain parts of Germany followed. In Bavaria, for example, only those who raped other men or who had sex with boys under 12 were prosecuted. But in all parts of Germany men could be imprisoned if they did something against public decency, a seemingly normal demand since having sex, for example, in the middle of a public street [homosexual or heterosexual sex], struck everyone as bad form. The law, in reality however, was diverted to cover whatever the police wanted it to cover. An example: a boy who related to another boy how he had been fucked--but well paid--in a park, was overheard by a woman who was shocked, a public act of indecency because the boys had spoken in public. The boy was found and jailed. But even this liberalism was revoked following several horrendous rapes of minors, and in 1871 laws were again reenacted in Germany against sodomy.

The population of Berlin exploded, from the 400,000 to 4 million in 1920. Berlin went from a city of open sewers to the first city ever electrified, with, in 1800, electric streetcars and lighting. It went from a city of open sewers to one of public toilets and baths, from the filthiest to the cleanest city in the world, infinitely more hygienic than London, Paris and N.Y. At the end of the 1400s in Florence the Office of the Night was formed to put an end to sodomy. The penalty was death but everyone got off with a slap on the wrist, except those who forced children to have sex. In 1885 Berlin established the Department of Homosexuals, proof of the growing number of gays. The police collected information and mug shots of homosexuals, and encouraged doctors and educators to study Berlin's unique sexual subculture, thanks to which reams of information concerning the sexuality of the times have come to us. In 1896 the name of the Department of Homosexuals was changed to Department of Homosexuals and Blackmailers. More money could be gained by pimps putting 14-year-old boys on the streets and then blackmailing the clients. In

1902 Friedrich Krupp, the Cannon King, committed suicide when blackmail led to the publication of his preference for Italian boys. For such a rich, powerful man to end his own life so young spoke volumes about being branded a homosexual, about the prevalence of blackmail and about the availability of underage lads. The department store magnate Hermann Israel killed himself on his yacht at age 40 when his companion blackmailed him. Before dying Israel turned the boy's threatening letters over to the police. The lad was sentenced to two months imprisonment. Victims of blackmail numbered in the hundreds, two of whom were well-known jurists, one who shot his blackmailer when he literally didn't have a cent left to pay him off. In 1902 a 28-year-old ophthalmologist committed suicide when his card was found in a boy's jacket and the ophthalmologist was threatened with a trial. At the time, it was established that a third of Berlin's homosexuals were being blackmailed. But as Berlin's reputation for male prostitution bloomed, johns from all over Europe flocked to the world's greatest center of boys.

Although boy whorehouses would number in the hundreds in pre-W.W.I years, the beginnings in the very early 1900s were rudimentary, where everyone from a club owner to a tobacconist could use a backroom for financial gain, recruiting hustlers and male trade from off the streets. Any man could have a room and rent out his boys, as pimps have since the beginning of time. And as the boys were often twelve to fifteen, their suitors could be either blackmailed or robbed while busy with their young prey. Any schoolboy or shop boy, any servant or thief, sailor or soldier, could round off monthly earnings by playing innocent or butch or changing into drag.

Rich men like Krupp, as stated, were openly blackmailed, or writers would threaten to publish tell-all books if they didn't pay up. Some hustlers trailed likely johns and then, catching hold of them, accused them of soliciting and threatened to call the police. Robert Beachy in his wonderful *Gay Berlin* (2014) tells us that this at times ended in jail terms for the blackmailer, and the boys could be clobbered by the men they pursued, especially if, as in one case, the target was a bullish butcher, but these brave citizens were most probably the vast minority.

What happened next was pretty much inexplicable to rationalists. As clubs gained in number so did those who took advantage of johns, robbing and blackmailing them. More and more targets were out-of-town Germans [as city dwellers had become streetwise], many well-off merchants and industrialists. This in turn inspired more boys to go to Berlin, which in turn drew still more men seeking youths. Soon the British came, followed by Americans. Those who sought and bought sex returned home to flaunt the merits of Berlin's boys, often hung, often highly-sexed lads who, because of their growing numbers, cost less and less. The minority of men robbed and otherwise extorted turned more and more to the police who had such complete files on the boys, largely thanks to the effective Chief of Police Leopold von Meerscheidt-Hüllessem, that the lads were often apprehended and the stolen goods retrieved. This made great copy for newspapers, thanks to which more and more foreigners learned about Berlin's boys. More rent and johns flocked to the new gay oasis, in [small] part responsible for its population exploding to 4 million, including [according to one estimate] a pre-W.W. II total of 170 boy bordellos. More than an oasis, Berlin became an earthly heaven because every variation of sex was represented, because beer and liquor flowed, and because of hugely successful floorshows, as seen in Isherwood's *Cabaret*.

German boys practiced sports that kept their bodies trim, and naked sunbathing took place around lakes, along rivers and even in public swimming pools, thanks to which the boys were beautifully tanned. Many foreign lads, especially the English, the opposite of this, hesitated to denude themselves. German boys tended to be masculine, they liked to exercise and they liked to show off their toned bodies. Their smiles were often ravaging, they enjoyed roughhousing, and sexually were highly experienced. Compared to the English they were animals, studs to British boarding-school lads who, among themselves, were used to lying on their stomachs in passive wait of penetration. Of his intimate friend Pieps, Auden said, "I like sex and Pieps likes money. It's a good exchange."

Kiosks were literally flooded with dozens of publications, and the kiosk owners didn't hesitate to have some pinned open, showing nude males. In 1930 Berlin had 280,000 tourists a year, among which were 40,000 Americans. There were believed to have been 100,000 rent-boys, all out for money to live on or pocket change, many of whom were believed to have been heterosexual. And they were cheap, especially soldiers and sailors going for 50 pfennig. Thomas Mann discovered Berlin at age 17. Christopher Isherwood refused to spend more than 10 marks, dinner and a few drinks for his boys [although this was outrageously overpaying], W.H. Auden, in his diary, detailed his sexual encounters, and the architect Philip Johnson claimed to have learned German through the horizontal method.

Sex was tame in some high-class clubs [although no-holds-barred was the rule in boy whorehouses]. At the urinals boys flashed their wares, and at tables boys allowed johns to put their hands through their pockets, which had been cut away inside to allow seizure of the lads' dicks. Lederhosen was popular in the butch places Isherwood frequented, showing off boys' suntanned thighs. Isherwood was said to have had 500 during the time he was there, from 1929 to 1933. The beautiful boys were in private clubs and in private hands, wealthy hands, hands that could offer far more than Isherwood's ten marks, even if ten marks were extremely generous for what was available. The boys who went with Isherwood thought he was fabulously rich because they were fabulously lacking in the attributes that would place them in an entirely different class. That said, Isherwood wrote that there were so many postulants that he always found a handsome lad for the night. [All lads have to start somewhere. Even gorgeous Alain Delon began as a rent-boy in Montmartre (14) and Paul Newman opened his fly for any director who promised him a role (27).

Boys of quality in pre-W.W. II Berlin were in private hands,
not Auden and Isherwood's.

Then, as today, coke was ubiquitous, except that it had just been invented, by Albert Niemann, and was not only fully accepted, it was recommended by Freud to his patients. Klaus Mann preferred heroine but also took cocaine, said to circulate like cigarettes, and everyone was into other drugs, like morphine and opium. After using coke one writer said, "I felt exhilarated, strong and capable of going on without tiredness." Some doctors and researchers believed that men became homosexual when using cocaine, that the drug was the cause, while most believed that coke simply lessened inhibitions, which liberated men with latent homosexuality or bisexuality to free themselves from self-imposed restraints. Cocaine helped one become more sociable and less shy.

The sudden liberation from fear that followed W.W.I created a state of euphoria, when men realized that they had survived, which was far from the case for the millions, *millions*, whose bodies nurtured the soil of France and Germany, where acre after acre of tombstones are now grassy havens of peace, and whose memorials, with their interminable lists of names, are sentinels at the entrance of every single village and town. The liberation from such a destiny fed an explosion of gaiety, an explosion of relief that life could now resume, and that at the very minimum it had to be seized, cherished and drained, like a perfect liquor, to the last drop.

Such was the catalyst of the Roaring Twenties. Such was the boom in expectations that fired the world's most sexually liberated capital, pre-W.W. II Berlin. The choice of Berlin was no accident, as the roots of sexual emancipation went far deeper, so deep in fact that many historiographers refer to the city as having *invented* homosexuality.

Before the 1800s men were omnisexual. The Greeks bedded women but preferred men. The Romans were, sexually, largely half and half. Christianity made loving one's male neighbor a sin, and the same-sex part of omnisexuality (3) largely went underground, with the exception of the Renaissance where it was common for men to seduce boys age 9 or older. Purely homosexual men like de Vinci and Michelangelo were rare; most others, like Cellini, extolled the beauty of boys although Cellini claimed that his best night ever had been with a girl (30).

In the 1800s Victorian men who preferred only boys gathered in places of male prostitution, the molly houses, in parks and outside barracks (10), and formed associations like the Bloomsbury Set (16) and the Apostles (21), although the root of boy love was in the major prep schools and colleges where dormitories were jaded with no-holds-barred orgies, absolute sanctuaries where lads could discover, among themselves, their degree of homosexuality, heterosexuality or bisexuality (4).

Germany was the hub of homosexuality, with sociological investigations under the likes of Magnus Hirschfeld, and kiosks showed the works of soft-core pornographers like Adolf Brand. France permitted homosexuality from 1791 and the Netherlands soon followed. Prussia was a fertile soil for male-male sex, as Germany is today, along with America and what has always been a boy-paradise, Italy, since the arrival of Trojan Aeneus (24), eternal Italy, the eternal Mecca for homosexual Germans and Brits even before Byron (10).

Germany is called the homeland of homosexuality because where the French, the Italians and the British decided to let sleeping dogs lie, the Germans rose up against statutes forbidding certain forms of sexuality, investing huge amounts of time in newspaper articles and conferences and magazines and organizations, like Hirschfeld's, to have the homophobic laws overturned. Luckily the press had been freed by Frederick the Great, who had even allowed Voltaire to publish the list of his male lovers.

Freud and William Reich

Freud felt that confirmed homosexuals could not be changed because they in no way suffered from their being gay. People who want to change their sexuality for societal reasons [like the insults he hears daily in a looker-room situation] can never change their orientation, and indeed, Freud would accept them for analysis only if they were suffering neurotically from being homosexual, in which case he would accept them as patients but only to help them accept themselves as they were. Freud said that the whys and wherefores of homosexuality remained the greatest mystery of his life.

William (Wilhelm) Reich (1897–1957), worked closely with Freud. His name was yelled out by students during the May '68 Student Revolt in Paris because he encouraged coeducation, with the sexes allowed to mingle and have intercourse when they desired to do so, as well as fostering omnisexuality (3). His life defies belief, and concerns us because he was born in Austria-Hungary [now the Ukraine] and had extremely liberal views concerning homosexuality. In his diaries he told of trying to have sex with the family maid with whom he slept in the same bed, at age 4, and at age 11 he was fucking the family servants daily. He started visiting brothels at age 15 and daily at age 17. When he found out his mother was sleeping with one of his tutors he threatened to reveal all to his father if she didn't allow him to fuck her. She refused, he did as he threatened to do, and she killed herself [he was 13].

Reich fought in W.W.I and at age 22, while studying medicine, he met Freud who was so impressed by him that he gave Reich patients to analyze. Reich was accused of making his first patient pregnant and then of killing her in a botched abortion attempt. The girl's mother protested to the authorities and Reich claimed she did so because he had refused her sexual advances. She too committed suicide. Reich's biographer, Myron Sharaf, claimed Reich ordered other women and even his wives to have abortions, perhaps to spare him the cost of raising the children.

Reich around age 25.

He became a medical doctor and then studied neuropsychiatry under Nobel Prize Winner in Medicine Julius Wagner von Jauregg. He became an assistant director of Freud's Vienna clinic in 1924 at age 27. He gave seminars and his eloquence was described as enchanting and spellbinding. His presence and domination over others was, he himself wrote, "like a shark in a pond of carps."

He wrote erudite books extremely well received, especially by his mentor Freud. He championed "orgasmic potency", stating that psychic health depended on the full discharge of the libido, that was "not just fucking but included all of the excitation leading up to fucking" [his exact words]. "The more intense the preliminaries, the more intense is the orgasm, and the more satisfying and fulfilling the release." In this he seems to have been criticized, labeled the "prophet of a better orgasm", the "founder of genital utopia" and the man who believed that an orgasm was the solution to every neurosis.

He opened a number of clinics that gave free medical advice in contraception as well as psychoanalytic counseling, and he joined the Communist Party. His clinic became mobile. He drove into the suburbs and parks with a team of psychoanalysts and doctors, with advice, counsel and contraceptives. Even children were included in his effort at enlightenment, and teenagers encouraged to fully explore their sexuality. His promotion of teenage sex eventually got him excluded from the Danish Communist Party.

Reich had experiments using students in which they kissed and touched while Reich measured their body reactions on an oscillograph. One such student was the future chancellor Willy Brandt. Reich and his son spent a great deal of time looking for UFOs and in America he invented the orgone accumulator in which the buyer--for example Norman Mahler [who owned several], Ginsberg, J.D. Salinger, Jack Kerouac and many others--sat naked and were cured of cancer.

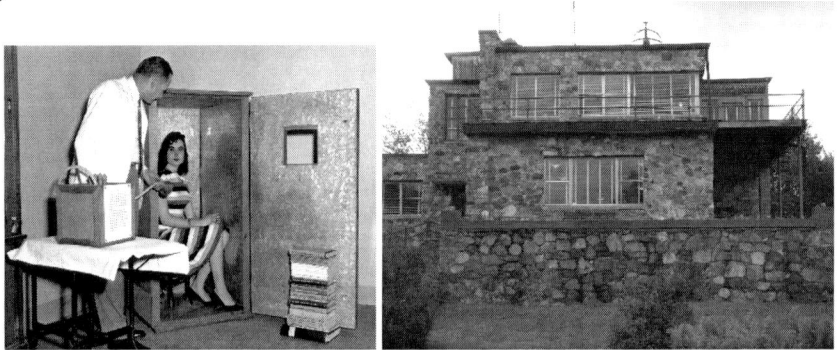

His Orgone Accumulator. His museum in Orgonon Maine

Imprisoned for being a charlatan, Reich was found dead in his cell, apparently of a heart attack.

Freud and his thoughts on homosexuality are perplexing. On the one hand his belief that we all start out as bisexuals, that homosexuality is too rooted in a man to be altered, and that homosexuals are every bit as virile as heterosexuals, seems sound. Whereas, on the other hand, he was deeply interested in Eugen Steinach's attempt to replace a homosexual's testicles with those of a heterosexual, making him straight, which is strange to say the least.

In fact, Freud's clearest view on the subject was in response to a letter from a woman who feared for her son: ''I gather from your letter that your son is a homosexual. I am most impressed by the fact that you do not mention this term yourself in your information about him. May I question you why you avoid it? Homosexuality is assuredly no advantage, but it is nothing to be ashamed of, no vice, no degradation; it cannot be classified as an illness; we consider it to be a variation of the sexual function. Many highly respectable individuals of ancient and modern times have been homosexuals, several of the greatest men among them. [Plato, Michelangelo, Leonardo da Vinci, etc]. It is a great injustice to persecute homosexuality as a crime--and a cruelty, too.

''What analysis can do for your son runs in a different line. If he is unhappy, neurotic, torn by conflicts, inhibited in his social life, analysis may bring him harmony, peace of mind, full efficiency, whether he remains homosexual or not.''

The complexity of why a boy becomes homosexual

is such that psychiatrists seem to throw up their hands, ceding their places to those scientists in search of a "gay gene" that will miraculously explain it all. In the lack of such a discovery it's easy to give credence to those who think that homosexuality is largely based on Narcissism: self-love that leads one to choose an object that resembles himself, a concept easy to understand, but in that case, in today's "me" world, shouldn't there be far more homosexuals than there are, because what boy isn't in love with himself? What boy doesn't kiss his reflection in the mirror? What boy hasn't gotten hard admiring the beauty of his own body?

Magnus Hirschfeld

In 1885 the Berlin police commissioner Leopold von Meerscheidt-Hüllessem founded the Department of Homosexuals to keep track of them for the seemingly benevolent reason of freeing homosexuals from blackmail and the resultant suicides. He personally conducted tours for the rich through the gay dives of the city, where he knew the boys by name, tours that perhaps brought him money from those who were out to do a little slumming because he eventually killed himself when caught accepting bribes from a banker he was protecting from accusations of rape.

It was largely thanks to Meerscheidt-Hüllessem's *laissez-faire* attitude that homosexual restaurants, clubs, bars, indoor and outdoor dance halls and costume balls flourished, and homosexual playgrounds alongside rivers, lakes, canals and railways became popular for immediate consumption. Sexual liberation in Berlin was a drawing power, but equally so was the fact that there was something for everyone: cross-dressers, their cheeks rouged and their eyebrows plucked; sadists paid to stomp on the likes of masochistic Auden; virile hustlers who let johns feel their yards through their trousers, often of military fabrication as soldiers and sailors were well aware of the appeal of their uniforms and positioned themselves just outside their barracks or along the Unter den Linden, in the Tiergarten Park and Friedrichstrasse, known for its prostitutes, and Berlin's Broadway, the Ku'damm. The more one aged, the more one was obliged to exchange the warmth and ambience of clubs and bars in search of johns outside, in parks and along streets, in bath houses and swimming pools.

Magnus Hirschfeld was ostracized by most homosexuals because of his interest in effeminacy, lesbians and cross-dressers, all of which undermined a homosexual man's image of himself as being more virile than straights because homosexuals changed partners more often and had sex more often. This was largely true because men were out for an orgasm, preferably in parks, forests and the like [outdoor sex is always an added stimulant], unions that could rapidly increase in the number of participants out for the same thrill. There was no convincing, as was a necessity with women, although heterosexuals maintained that such rites boosted one's lust, while homosexuals knew that what really excited a man were a few minutes with an unknown male, discovering the mysterious contents shielded by the buttons of a pair of trousers, in places as dangerously exposed as possible.

Magnus Hirschfeld (1868–1935) was a sexologist who practiced in Berlin. He founded the Scientific Humanitarian Committee with others in 1897, the two-fold interest of which was 1) to abrogate the 1871 law criminalizing homosexuality and 2) to try to convince people that thanks to scientific understanding hostility to homosexuals would eventually be eliminated.

Hirschfeld's work was inspired by a military officer who committed suicide on the eve of his wedding, preferring death to what would be required on his honeymoon night, an epiphany for Hirschfeld, Beachy relates in his *Gay Berlin*.

Alas, Hirschfeld believed that homosexuality was a debility (†) and that homosexuals were effeminate, thus provoking a schism in his group and the formation of a second society, founded by those who believed that male-male love was another form of virile manliness. [† Light-years from Tim Cooke, President of Apple, who said: ''I consider being gay among the greatest gifts God has given me.'']

Dubbed the Einstein of sex, Hirschfeld opened the Institute for Sexual Research in the liberal Weimar Republic in 1919, that housed a Museum of Sex and had some 50 rooms, one of which was occupied for a time by Christopher Isherwood and visited by W.H. Auden, André Gide and Sergei Eisenstein. There was a museum with sex toys and walls plastered with photos of nudes, presumably there for sexual education, and lots of men dressed as women and women as men, both in photos and live as visitors. Teas were offered at the Institute, reigned over by Hirschfeld and his lover Karl Giese. Bar hopping at night was included, so that in one way or another one could meet and mate with whomever one wished, back "home" at the Institute. For those passing through like Isherwood the occasions to meet boys, the private rooms and stacks of pornography, made the Institute a lad's wet dream.

The Institute was manned by doctors, interns and students working on their Ph.Ds., and gave sexual instruction on birth control, venereal diseases and offered hormonal treatments and the first tries at transsexual surgery. In one operation a man who wanted to become a woman had his penis sort of pushed inside-out into a cavity, but when he later fell in love with a woman the surgery was reversed, with supposedly satisfying results; the patient, at any rate, went on to become a pathologist, recounts Beachy. Hirschfeld established 64 degrees of sexuality, from masculine heterosexual males to feminine homosexual males, with transsexuals somewhere along the line.

There was never-ending, at times extremely catty, philosophical, medical and scientific disagreements between all the men involved in the sexual research, especially those who foamed at the mouth when Hirschfeld called them an effeminate third sex. Relations were therefore far from a long, calm river, with, indeed, some furious rapids, especially when some men stole the boyfriends of other researchers.

The more Hirschfeld gained in renown the more he inspired jealously, especially from those who vomited his emphasis on homosexuals being a third girly-like sex, as well as the attention he paid to cross-dressers and androgynes. His enemies considered themselves equal to all other virile males, equal to the Ancient Greeks and their relations centered on men's love for boys. Hirschfeld favored bisexuality due to Darwin's law that heterosexuality flourished because heterosexuals procreated while homosexuals didn't, although most English homosexuals did marry when exposed to the societal pressures found in Victorian England, and in the States today men like politicians haven't a snowball's chance in Hell of survival if they are outed, and the best way to not be outed is to reproduce [ditto for actors].

The extremely rich history of the German contribution to Roaring Twenties' homosexuality included the following men:

Sascha Schneider

Rudolf Karl Alexander Schneider (1870–1927) was a German painter and sculptor. He lived with his lover, the painter Hellmuth Jahn, but had to flee to Florence when Jahn blackmailed him, threatening to have him arrested for homosexuality. He traveled widely with his new lover, Robert Speis. For unknown reasons Sascha then financed a voyage for Jahn to Egypt and they met a final time in Florence where Sascha's newest lover, Daniel Stepanoff, turned Jahn into the police because he continued to blackmail Sascha. In 1918 Sascha returned to Germany and opened up a bodybuilding gymnasium called the Kraft-Kunst from which he recruited the models for his art [an admittedly genial way of procuring boys, as far as I know unique in the history of artists]. He died at age 57 of diabetes.

Sascha Schneider's *Peace on Earth* and unnamed painting.

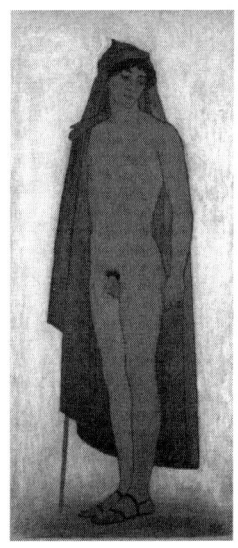

Youth in a Blue Coat.

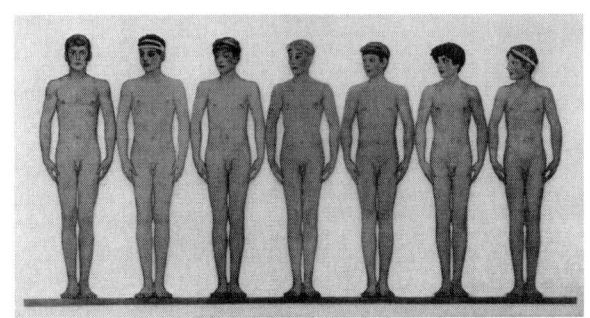

Schneider's *Gymnasium*.

John Henry Mackay

John Henry Mackay (1864–1933) was taken to Germany by his well-off mother at the death of his Scottish father when the boy was two. Rebellious and a poor student, his early love affairs were with boys his age, 14 to 17, and although he grew older his preference for adolescent lads did not.

An anarchist, his best-known homosexual work is *The Hustler* [*Der Puppenjung--The Boy-Doll*]. His poems were published in *Der Eigene* and he broke with Hirschfeld over Hirschfeld's belief that homosexuals were third-sex-effeminates. Mackay extolled masculinity but unlike many gays he found nothing superior in the love of males to heterosexuals' preferences for girls.

He wrote a series of books called *Nameless Love*, a potpourri of his poems, stories, essays and philosophical beliefs. Judged obscene, his editor--never giving up Mackay's name as the author--was found guilty, but Mackay paid the fines and court costs.

He died in 1933, three months after Hitler's ascension to power, ten days after the Nazi book-burning festival, which saw the destruction of his works [some claim he committed suicide, but this is far from certain].

Max Liebermann

Max Liebermann (1847–1935) studied law, philosophy and then art in Paris and the Netherlands. He was a medic in the Franco-Prussian War. His Jewish father had been a banker whose wealth allowed Liebermann to collect French Impressionist art. He gave solo exhibitions, one at the Prussian Academy in whose ranks he was elected at age 51. Forced out in 1933 by the Nazis, he died in his sleep in 1935. Ordered to a concentration camp in 1943, his bedridden wife committed suicide.

Liebermann's *Im Schwimmbad.*

Glyn Philpot

The British painter Glyn Philpot (1884–1937) is of interest to us because he lived in pre-W.W. II Berlin where he was greatly influenced by the ease of sex with boys, which liberated his painting to the extent that it included male nudes. He joined the Royal Fusiliers where he met Vivian Forbes, described as witty, charming and unstable, the love of Philpot's life despite their union portrayed as tumultuous. Philpot was buried on the 22nd of December 1937 and on the 23rd Forbes took his own life.

Vivian Forbes in Philpot's *Boy with Rabbit* and his *St. Sebastian*.

Adolf Brand

Born in Berlin, Adolf Brand (1874 – 1945) founded *Der Eigene, The Special One* [or *The Unique*], the first magazine to celebrate love between men.

Der Eigene and *Der Eigene* boys.

Brand, like Paul Friedländer, believed that males were not feminine, nor did they form a third effeminate sex. They were, to the contrary, the peak of masculinity. He advocated nudism and outdoor living, love between men and adolescent boys, taking Greece, like Friedländer, as the ultimate aspiration. Both Friedländer and Brand believed that men were bisexual, and both married. Brand served in W.W.I and wedded a nurse with whom he set up a *ménage-à-trois* with Max Miede who appeared nude in *Der Eigene*.

Max Miede

Der Eigene published--other than nudes--poetry, prose and political manifestos, often in support of Weimar liberality. The number of subscribers is unknown, but estimated at 1,500 per issue. There were classified ads, like: student, 22, seeks a real man for friendship ... letter with photograph obligatory, or this: male, 29, seeks an exchange of ideas with a student, very pure, 20–25.

In 1933 Brand wrote that the Nazis had a "hangman's rope in their pockets." In revenge they raided his home and workshop, destroying everything he had concerning homosexuality, reducing him to extreme poverty. He and his family died in 1945, victims to Allied bombings.

Accused of being anti-Semitic, in reality Brand disowned all religions that set up obstacles between men and their rights to love boys. It's true that for him whites were superior and women intellectually inferior, but he was against the exploitation of women and advocated their right to relieve themselves of their burdensome virginity when the occasion presented itself. The focal point of his life was best summed up in his own words: "The right of self-determination over body and soul is the most important basis of all freedom."

Brand did not only defend Greek love, he wished to bring Ancient Greece to Berlin in its entirety. He founded an organization called, modestly, the Community of the Special, that had regular meetings dubbed symposiums after Brand's conception of what went on in the Athenian agora. The Community was prone to nature hikes in the nude, and was built on the principle of love between a man and the boy the man would better through education, and this until the boy was old enough to marry, after which the boy, now a man, would find a boy he could, in turn, love and educate--Greece at its most classic (31).

His boys eventually married, as he did himself, which in no way stopped him from having multiple lovers, a perfect life only an allied bomb could put an end to.

Wilhelm von Gloeden

Brand published pictures by Wilhelm von Gloeden:

Sicilian boys by Wilhelm von Gloeden.

Wilhelm von Gloeden had gone to the island of Sicily for his health. His guide was a 16-year-old donkey driver with whom he spent a night in such ecstasy, he wrote, that he bought a villa and hired local 13- and 14-year-olds to staff it. The boys' parents competed in having their lads work for him as he paid well, he took scrupulous care of their health and needs, he turned over the royalties from the photos he took of them, and he provided dowries so that his favorites could marry. His character was such that everyone sought him out. His orgies became famous and visitors to them were said to have been in the hundreds [presumably not all at the same time]. Frederick von Krupp was one, who later tried to recreate Taormina on Capri. When his homosexuality came to light, Krupp put a bullet in his head, although his death was masked as a heart attack. Gloeden was noted as the first man to use filters and body make-up, said to have been composed of milk, glycerin, olive oil and perfume. He left his negatives to his lover, Il Moro, whom he had "known" at age 13. He at times worked with his cousin, Guglielmo Plüschow, an avid boy-lover said to have been less talented and more stilted in his posing of the lads. Some people at Taormina, today, claim that the origin of their wealth is a heritage from the sums given to their grandsons.

Il Moro and Gloeden.

Friedrich Radszuweit

Friedrich Radszuweit (1876–1932) was a Berlin homosexual activist who published mildly erotic magazines and books he himself wrote. Radszuweit published *Die Freundschaft* from 1919 until the reign of the Nazis in 1933. It was by far the most successful publication, selling an estimated 15,000 copies at each printing, making Radszuweit rich, especially when this income was supplemented by ads from not only bars, cafés and clubs, but also from men's clothing shops, barbers and doctors whose discretion homosexuals relied on for anal disorders as well as, Beachy says, "throat rashes". Radszuweit founded the Theater of Eros, known for the homosexual content of its plays and deep kissing between male actors on stage. Like Adolf Brand, Radszuweit's brand of homosexuality included virile males only, with no place whatsoever for Hirschfeld's cross-dressing effeminates. Radszuweit differed sharply from Brand in his belief that males were entirely attracted to and satisfied by other males, which excluded bisexuality, and that boys were to be protected, which was not the case under Brand where boys were meant to be dominated by mature, responsible men. Radszuweit believed in Brand's assertion that only between males could one find the highest degree of moral strength, spiritual calm and sexual release.

His magazine *Männer*.

His lover was Martin Butzko, an active member of the Hitler Youth whom he adopted as his son. Martin-Butzko Radszuweit took over the publishing company when his "father" died in 1932, but the establishment was raided and destroyed by the Nazis in 1933. Hirschfeld's Institute and estate were destroyed at the same time and Hirschfeld himself died in France in 1935 at the age of 67, his faithful lover Giese presumably at his side.

Henry Gerber

Henry Gerber (1892–1972) was born in Bavaria and emigrated to America at age 21. When war broke out with Germany he was given the choice of being interned or of joining the American Army. He chose the Army and was sent to Coblenz for three years as a printer and proofreader. It was there he learned about Hirschfeld and became his acolyte, adopting, alas, Hirschfeld's idea that homosexuals were just naturally effeminate. Back in the States he worked at the post office in Chicago. He founded the first homosexual organization in America, the Society of Human Rights, the goal of which was: "to promote and protect the interests of people who by reasons of mental and physical abnormalities are abused and hindered in the legal pursuit of happiness which is guaranteed them by the Declaration of Independence." As homosexuals were the "mental and physical abnormalities" he defended, we can be grateful for the fact that the Society had an early death, in a way that was almost hilarious: He decided to limit the Society to exclusively homosexuals, apparently unaware that his vice-president had two children. The vice-president's wife called the police who put Gerber on trial *three times* for being a degenerate.

The charges were eventually dismissed but Gerber lost his life savings in lawyers' fees and the bribes it was necessary to pay out at the time [it being, after all, Chicago]. He was fired from the post office for "conduct unbecoming...."

He met up with an old army pal who suggested he reenlist, which he did, preparing magazines and recruiting publications for the Army Recruiting Bureau. He retired in 1945 and for the next thirty years was an active part of the N.Y. gay scene, also corresponding with groups around the country and in Germany. He entered the Soldiers' and Airmens' Home in Washington D.C. where he died at age 80 in 1972.

Although not a single rich Chicago homosexual offered Gerber a penny for his defense during his trial, they've made up for it since then. The Henry Gerber House where he had started the Society of Human Rights became an official Chicago Landmark in 2001 and then a National Historic Landmark, in 2015. Gerber was enrolled in the Chicago Gay and Lesbian Hall of Fame. Too bad that Gerber passed away far too soon to reap the rewards for his courage.

Thomas Mann

Thomas Mann's early years were exclusively homosexual, his first love and lover the schoolboy Armin Martins he immortalized in his book *Tonio Kröger*:

Thomas Mann and his first love Armin Martens, hero of Mann's book *Tonio Kröger*.

A second unnamed boyhood love is thought to have been the inspiration behind the hero of his *Magic Mountain*, Hans Castorp.

The love of his life was perhaps Paul Ehrenberg, a violinist and impressionist painter:

Paul Ehrenberg--with my apologies for the terrible image. Of his four years of love with Paul he wrote, ''I have lived and loved. I knew happiness, held in my arms he I longed for." To my mind the very aim of life. The *only* aim of life.

At age 53 he fell in love with Klaus Heuser, 17:

Klaus Heuser

And at age 75 he loved a young Zurich waiter, Franz Westermeier [no photo available], around whom he wrote *The Confessions of Felix Krull*.

Death in Venice, like his other books, reflected true-life experiences, this one taking place at the Grand Hôtel des Bains on the Lido of Venice in the summer of 1911. After *Death in Venice* came out the boy-hero of the book recognized himself and went wild, shouting out to one and all, "That's me! That's me!" Władysław Moes' story is of incidental interest. Born in 1900 [he died at age 88], Władysław Moes was at the Grand Hôtel des Bains in 1911 during a visit by Mann, who published his book in 1922. Władysław Moes was born into a Polish family of extremely rich industrialists. He lost everything with the Communist takeover and earned his living as a translator. In an interview to the Polish translator of Mann's works he said, "Even in

Venice they called me Adzio, and in the story I'm Tadzio, which is how the Master understood it.''

There are numerous theories as to why Thomas married, his many biographers suggest that his wife's family was rich and as a young writer he was poor, or that he wanted to punish himself for his homosexuality, or that he capitulated to convention, sacrificing his true nature in order to protect his public image.

Thomas Mann taught at Princeton before moving to California, and spent the last three years of his life in Switzerland.

[The full story of Mann's life, and that of his sons, is found in my book *German Homosexuality*.]

The Wandervogel Movement

The Wandervogel movement (1896–1933), a name most likely taken from Walt Whitman's ''Birds of Passage'', sprang up in Berlin when high school students turned their walks through the forests into an antibourgeois back-to-nature group based on hiking, swimming, camping, singing and storytelling, most often in tents or barns, in the nude. The conversations around campfires were on how to make Germany and Europe a better place. It was homoerotic, but only in the sense that male-male love was a simple, natural aspect of manhood. It gave meaning to a German boy's life, in which friendship and camaraderie became a cult. Around the year 1900 it had 26,000 members.

"A one-sided cultivation of the body is as wrong as the exclusive education of the intellect. One creates healthy, robust blockheads; the other flabby, bent scholars. The Golden Mean is a sound mind in a sound body." Wandervogel philosophy.

In 1931 Hans Blüher organized a subdivision of the Wandervogel, one for men only, based on male bonding. His movement was publicized by Adolf Brand's *Der Eigene*. Blüher based his ideas on male cohesion as shown through the Spartans (18) and the Sacred Band of Thebes (19), Hadrian and Antinous (29) and, of course, Wagner and his *Persifal*.

Homosexuality was a natural phenomenon in sexuality, as were other forms, so that exclusively homosexual attachments were in no way obligatory in Blüher's Wandervogel. But as the journalist Ludwig Lewisohn wrote in 1933, the Wandervogel was "the youth movement from which thousands of stormtroopers came, its ideology drenched through with homoerotic feeling *and practice*", my italics. The Wandervogel and all other youth movements were incorporated into the Hitler Youth in 1933.

''No young man should marry before he has seen his beloved in the nude, just as he sees his comrades in the nude. Nudism elevates the pleasure of every individual and the joy of our whole people in bodily strength and beauty.'' Adolf Brand.

The Wondervogel movement was influenced by Richard Ungewitters' books, all on nudism [naturalism today] which recommended going nude as a way of keeping healthy [clothes being the breeders of tuberculosis, maintained Ungewitters], especially as nudists were advised to do a lot of healthy hiking. Women could visually see the attributes of virile males, meaning a strengthening of the race because weaklings would not be chosen in reproduction. He wrote that exercising three times a day should be made obligatory.

Hans Blüher

Hans Blüher (1888–1955) started out in the Wandervogel at age 14 but received a dressing-down for homosexual activity. He met Wilhelm Jansen, a member of Hirschfeld's committee and he and Friedländer encouraged Blüher's homosexuality-- Blüher then 18--which was easy as Blüher had been making love with boys since puberty. He married, a passionless love known to boys on both sides of the Channel, the British too succumbing to bourgeois normality and societal demands. He adopted Freud's theory that we are all born innately bisexual, which comforted Blüher in his love of boys and later marriage. Blüher admitted one exception to bisexuality, that of ''super-virile homosexuals'' who have physical contacts with men only. For Blüher physical contacts between men were both positive and good. Blüher believed that friendship and erotic love were the norm between men, while Hirschfeld thought that heterosexuals could love men as friends only.

Blüher rightly claimed that before Christianity muddied the waters, love between men was a simple aspect of manhood, not a special condition of man.

Arno Breker

Arno Breker (1900–1991) was a German sculptor whose prizes, awarded by the Prussian Ministry of Culture, allowed him to live in Paris and Rome.

Breker and his *Alexander the Great* and *Seated Man.*

Called "Germany's Michelangelo" by the sculptor and painter Aristide Maillol, he was friends with Picasso, Jean Renoir, Albert Speer and Hitler, all of whom appreciated his muscular and flawlessly handsome Aryan sculptures. Although he escaped allied bombing, the occupation forces nonetheless destroyed nearly all of his *oeuvre*.

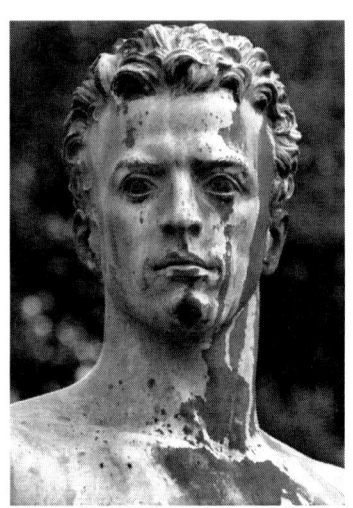

Young Man.

When offered work by Stalin, Breker declined with "One dictator was enough!" Rehabilitated, the Arno Breker Museum was inaugurated in 1985.

[The full history of what took place in Germany can be found in my book *German Homosexuality*.]

PART FOUR

LA BELLE EPOQUE

An Introduction

The Roaring Twenties was called the Belle Époque in France, where Montmartre cabarets swarmed with life in all its uninhibited forms, Toulouse-Lautrec recording it all in breathtaking art, the art itself a new form: Art Nouveau, inspired by natural forms, the curved lines of plants and flowers, never before seen colors, where Mistinguett exchanged Maurice Chevalier as lover for an artist aged 16, and Jean

Cocteau--the icon of the Belle Époque and, as such, the main contributor to this Part--enhanced films with the beauty of Jean Marias, as did Marcel Carné in *Drôle de Drame* with the erotic presence of Jean-Pierre Aumont. Diaghilev made Paris the ballet capital of Europe thanks to his lover Nijinsky, and Stravinsky astonished the world with his *Sacre du printemps,* as Diaghilev had commissioned him to do. Ravel rivaled Gide in the appreciation of Arab lads, and Genet blew smoke through a straw from one cell to another, the man on each side taking his individual pleasure.

The French Exposition Universelle of 1900.

French culture [meaning Paris] reigned supreme, French imperialism was unstoppable, and at the very gateway to America France's gift to the United States, the Statue of Liberty, warmly welcomed visitors and immigrants alike. As with the Greece of Pericles, where the elite was free to expound the ideal of democracy because they were themselves supported by slaves, so too was there an underclass during the Belle Époque, one that lived in misery and in slums, where homosexuality was somewhat of a leveler when the affluent and the literati reached down to choose an occasional lover, mostly temporarily although in Cocteau's case he adopted his boy, stating that he couldn't help all miners, the boy's milieu, but he would help *this* miner.

France was the center of haut couture and cuisine, where a chef, Auguste Escoffier, could rise in fame and fortune to become half-owner of the Ritz, while Ritz waiters provided Proust with the salacious material he would use in his book, as well as appeasing him sexually in one of the rooms reserved for dining and fucking, Proust wealthy enough to have advanced the funds for two male brothels, and offered one of his boys an airplane and his own Rolls-Royce to get him to the airport and back, a plane responsible for the boy's death.

Art Nouveau came into existence, visible today in museums and at the entrance of certain Paris Metro Stations, the metro which made travel easier, especially for the working classes [certain upper-class men had their own private railway train wagons, which freed them from first-class compartments]. The Metro allowed the classes to live at greater distances from each other, reinforcing the gulf between them. The period saw the rise of anarchism and political assassination, both rare in France [but with earth-shattering consequences in Russia]. The Dreyfus Affair was *the* scandal of the times, prior to the Roaring Twenties, revealing France's anti-Semitism, but gave Émile Zola an occasion to win immortality, although not a place in France's home of heroes, the Panthéon, a sad oversight.

Art Nouveau Metro.

What is amazing about Art Nouveau was that it created a new style of such immense beauty that Art Nouveau buildings, paintings, jewelry, furniture, ceramics, glass art and metalwork are today next to priceless. Artists who most appreciated Art Nouveau were Aubrey Beardsley, Pierre Bonnard, Émile Gallé in glass works, René Laliques in jewelry and in New York Louis Comfort Tiffany. The Exposition Universelle of 1900 was the showcase of Art Nouveau as was Le Train bleu, the restaurant of the Gare de Lion. Bicycles came into use in 1818, automobiles followed and Édouard Michelin invented tires. American ingenuity helped Paris become the City of Lights, followed by the telephone, but it was France that led the way in aviation and inaugurated the world's first air force in 1910. Léon Bouly and the Lumière brothers gave us the cinema, Pasteur vaccinated against rabies and introduced pasteurization, and a woman, Marie Curie, won the Nobel Prize for Physics in 1903 and Chemistry in 1911.

Belle Époque painting by Walter Crane and a Tiffany masterpiece.

The Moulin Rouge, its hallmark a red windmill on the roof, was built in 1889 at the foot of Montmartre hill, in the red-light district of Paris, Pigalle. It was here the abode of Genet and the place Alain Delon earned pocket money thanks to his beauty, just after his military service (14). The Moulin Rouge was home of the Can-Can, where girls raised their skirts to show off their panties, an era when a boy madly jerked off at the sight of a naked ankle. Yvette Guilbert danced and Toulouse-Lautrec immortalized her in paintings and on posters. It was the watering hole of Pigalle residents, workers, artists and foreigners, who rubbed shoulders and more *si affinité*. La Goulue put on an act and spread her legs for those who had the price of entry, and the student Bal des Quat'z'Arts had a scandalous procession that had a naked Cleopatra surrounded by equally naked young girls. Mistinguett made her début and Colette exchanged an infamous public kiss with the Duchess of Morny in 1907. The Moulin Rouge was destroyed by a fire in 1917 and reopened in 1921.

Le Moulin Rouge

Yvette Guilbert [1865-1944] was a Moulin Rouge singer, extremely lithe, who would perform standing perfectly still, motioning only with her long black gloves, raunchy words issuing from what chroniclers claim was the most virginal of faces, words that found their roots in a poverty-stricken childhood. She was the favorite artist of Toulouse-Lautrec, as well as Freud and George Bernard Shaw. She traveled widely, Germany, England and America, where she performed at Carnegie Hall. Hosts and hostesses vied for her appearances at private parties, one of whom was the future King Edward VII on the French Riviera. She married a doctor and turned to writing, penning two novels and a book on how to sing. She opened schools in singing in Paris and New York and was awarded the Legion of Honor. She died at age 79.

Yvette Guilbert by Toulouse-Lautrec.

La Goulue [Louise Weber, 1866-1929] was known as the Queen of Montmartre, and it was she who popularized the Can-Can by raising her skirt high over her waist, a red heart embroidered at the strategic spot of her white panties. She kicked off the hats of men who ventured within range of her feet and went from table to table, downing men's drinks, thusly winning the title of "glutton", *goulue* in French. Her mother was a laundress, as was La Goulue from her earliest childhood. She borrowed the dresses of her clients and danced in front of mirrors, and from age 16 the dresses and her daring style of dancing were seen in cabarets around Pigalle. She was taken on at the Moulin Rouge where Pierre-Auguste Renoir saw to it that she earned extra money by posing for painters and photographers, generally nude, all of which made her the highest-paid performer of her day [and costly *private* entertainer]. Alcohol and age wrecked their havoc and she eventually survived by selling peanuts, cigarettes and matches on Montmartre street corners, hugely overweight, unrecognizable.

La Goulue by Toulouse-Lautrec and photographed.

The Folies Bergère, named after the nearby rue Bergère [shepherdess], offered everything from operettas to gymnastics, nudity introduced in 1918, and in 1936 Josephine Baker stunned Paris dancing naked except for a string of artificial bananas around her midsection. Baker's life and open bisexuality were entirely exceptional. Obliged to scavenger for food in garbage cans, sleeping on cardboard boxes, she married a first time at age 13, a second at age 15. Street-corner dancing for money, she found a place in a chorus line that eventually played in Paris. Called the "Bronze Venus", the "Creole Goddess" and the "Black Pearl", she won fame at the Folies Bergère, but it was for her role in the French resistance during

W.W. II, gleaning information during her soirées and from the huge number of people she met, as well as her harboring French resistance fighters at her home in the South of France, that she was given the Croix de guerre and the Légion d'honneur from the hands of de Gaulle himself, before being asked to replace Martin Luther King as head of the Civil Rights Movement after his assassination, an offer she turned down for fear of something happening to her children. She married a French industrialist, her third but not last husband, and renounced her American citizenship in favor of France, her first love, she said, Paris being her second [or vice-versa], that she exulted in her famous song *"J'ai deux amours"*. She entertained the troops in North Africa, adopted 12 children, and in 1951 sang before 100,000 in Harlem, before receiving a standing ovation in 1973 at Carnegie Hall. She died of a cerebral hemorrhage at age 68.

Mistinguett [Jeanne Florentine Bourgeois, 1875-1956] was a signer, actress and dancer, known for songs like *Ça c'est Paris* and *Mon homme*, but equally for her love affair with Maurice Chevalier. She went the length and width of Europe when he was made a prisoner during the First World War, taking on the role of official spy for the French government. It was finally with the help of Spanish King Alphonse XIII that she arranged the liberation of her lover. When they broke up she fell in love with 16-year-old Charles Gesmar, she 41, whom he called Mama. Charles Gesmar, 1900-1928, would be famous today had he lived longer. Many believe that it was in huge part thanks to his posters and the costumes he designed that helped Mistinguett win her popularity, as she had never been described as particularly beautiful. "Everyone copied his designs," said Mistinguett, "and he would just say, 'Who cares! I have plenty of other ideas' ", which was the case. Orders for his costumes were coming in from all over Europe, especially Berlin and Vienna, and he was making huge amounts of money, "that he spent as if it would burn him, and if he didn't get rid of it he'd go up in flames," claimed Mistinguett. He would give a hundred francs when he took a taxi, "never less," she concluded.

Mistinguett with Chevalier, showing off her legs, and a poster designed by her 16-year-old artist/lover Charles Gesmar.

Homosexuality had a leveling effect, uniting the

bourgeoisie and the lower classes, but voices began to rise protesting that it was this mixture that was responsible for the weakening of the nation. How could a country remain strong when a prince was coupling with a vagabond, a count with an apache: the name used during the Belle Époque to describe young men from the popular classes, delinquents and criminals, at times pimps, at times hustlers, the word coming directly from what Europeans new of Geronimo and his uncivilized, cruel Indians. A prince was shown in a cartoon kissing the feet of youngsters, totally submissive to their hidden intimate charms. It was exactly this lack of virility that had led to France's defeat before the Prussians, as well as a drop in natality, because sperm was being lost between male buttocks, not invested in child-producing vaginas. This exact same complaint took place in Sparta when its population dangerously declined (18), and the great Augustus never tired of telling the Roman aristocracy that their role was to marry and produce children (35).

The centers where homosexuality was practiced changed after George-Eugène Haussman destroyed the myriad of streets and alleys in favor of today's large boulevards, work started in 1854. Before Haussman the streets were less lighted, the alleys so dark one couldn't see one's hand before his face. They were ideal arteries for robbers, and in the morning the dead--from brawls, murders and thefts--were collected for burial in common pits [thrown into the Seine in earlier times]. Rebellion was easy thanks to easily dressed barricades, and revolts and strikes were repressed with difficulty. Sexually they were paradise, where any alcove, cul-desac, doorway and arcade sufficed for a rapid exchange of mutual orgasms. The parks where men met were the same as under Louis XIV, headed by the Tuileries and Palais Royal, but during the Belle Époque these two were largely replaced by the Invalides, the Champ de Mars, the gardens of the Luxembourg, Parc Manceau and the Champs-Elysees with it trees and bushes and urinals, supplemented by bars, restaurants, cafés and baths, massage parlors and discrete male brothels. Heterosexual whorehouses also catered to men looking for boys, and amidst the largely heterosexual-oriented cliental the owner would send out for a boy who didn't mind sodomizing a man when the price was right. Pornography could be had but not in the open as in kiosks in Berlin (17), where magazines were pinned open, showing dicks erotic even at rest, often more so, although there were, for the moment, no bars and restaurants for the exclusive use of homosexuals in the French capital, as there were in Berlin. The boys the men sought out were often different too, and although many clients wanted virile men, especially in uniform, they were not against boy-dandies, while in Berlin lederhosen over tanned thighs was guaranteed to stimulate the blood, the inner pocket cut away so a man could hand-measure a boy's potential, the price extremely low because so many lads, many heterosexual, were out for a few extra coins (17). Urinals were a Parisian singularity, 4,000 in 1904 [!], where mutual masturbation took place in the twinkling of an eye. At the time there existed even cubicles where men could piss without being spied on, but these soon became glory holes so popular that even when the holes were sealed with cement, even when they were welded shut, they were back in use a week later, the purpose being fellations and intercourse when a mouth was replaced by an anus.

Examples of individual urinals.

Montmartre was the major center of drugs, prostitution and crime, the epicenter of Bohemian lifestyle, where morphine, opium and cocaine were bought, sold and used *sur place*. It had its first backrooms, in advance of New York and Berlin, Berlin where homosexuality was far more open than Paris but where overt sexual acts remained largely invisible because punished by the law. Two male brothels were paid for by Proust, and others shot throughout the city: the Hôtel de Mont-Blanc, the Hôtel des Bords de Rhins and the Hôtel de Madrid were among the most notorious (14).

The quays of the Seine were as visited as urinals, because back then they were unlit. We don't know much about private weddings among homosexuals during the Belle Époque, but they did take place, performed by a friend who'd dress up as a priest, the ceremony followed by a banquette. During one marriage a boy, age 16, was described as a *"très jolie petite merveille,"* a truly cute wonder. His husband was said to have been very rich.

A Belle Époque glass window and painting by Adele Bloch-Bauer.

Cocteau

As said, Jean Cocteau [1889-1963] best represented the Roaring Twenties. He was a *touche-à-tout*, writer, designer, playwright, film director and artist, his sketches of lascivious male nudes especially prized in gay circles [today included]. His father was a lawyer who committed suicide when Cocteau was 9, something that boys never recover from, and Cocteau was no exception. At age 11 he entered the Lycée Condorcet where his love for and sexual relations with Pierre Dargelos [no pictures available] would be the backdrop of Cocteau's entire *oeuvre*.

He admired Pierre Dargelos's animal beauty and desperately wished to be like him, especially as Cocteau was himself judged so physically inadequate he was excluded from military service. Although he had certainly "known" other boys, his earliest fantasy remained Pierre Dargelos, the memory of whom served for the sketches in his *Livre blanc*. "I've always preferred the strong sex that I can legitimately call the beautiful sex", he wrote, ["*J'ai toujours aimer le sex fort que je trouve légitime d'appeler le beau sexe*"]. He took part in plays at the Lycée Condorcet, along with the wonderful future actor Pierre Fresnay. Cocteau tried to pass his *baccalauréat* exam three times but failed, a rite of passage for students in France, passed today by around 80% of the those who take it. He had always been a mediocre student but thanks to his mother's wealth he would never lack for funds.

He discovered music halls early, and at age 16 lost his heterosexual cherry to a singer who told him she'd loved being in his arms and his being in her ["*J'étais heureuse hier dans tes bras de te sentir là, dans moi*"]. Later Cocteau wrote that the experience hadn't been at all the same for him, and that in shame he'd withdrawn from her like a knife ["*de honte et sortait d'elle comme un couteau*"]. He never explained why he'd felt shame in doing to the girl what his well-off friends were regularly doing to singers and actresses.

Cocteau hitched his wagon to a well-known homosexual actor of the times, Édouard de Max, who had him take part in plays, one in which he was dressed as the homosexual emperor Héliogabale (34), dressed so shamefully that Sarah Bernhardt herself said to the boy, "If I were your mother I'd send you home to bed!" Max arranged a presentation of Cocteau's poetry on the Champs-Elysees, and invited plenty of his friends to provide the claque, thusly assuring Cocteau's success. Always effeminate, Cocteau now copied the likes of Max and, especially, the dandy of them all, Oscar Wilde. Mamma Cocteau paid for it all, as she would until her death in 1943.

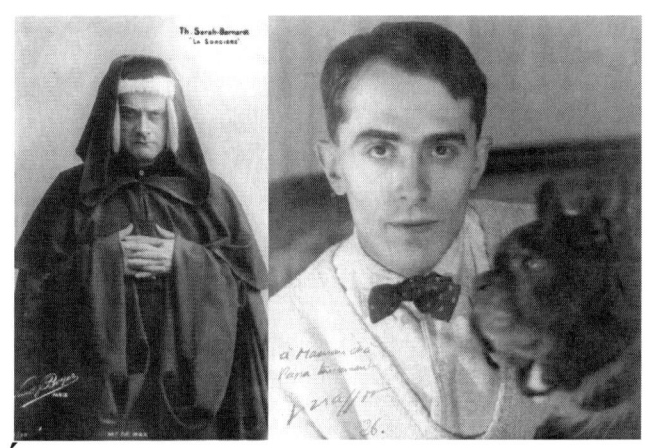

Édouard de Max and Pierre de Massot.

Any boy known to be one of Max's lads was deemed "damned". Max, 1869-1924, was of Romanian origin and considered a *joli garcon* [which may have been the case when young]. The very great actors in France became known as *les monstres sacrés*, of which Max, Sarah Bernhardt, Raimu, Louis Jouvet and Harry Baur were the most popular. His cigarettes were inscribed with his name, and his wealth was legendary. The love of his life, Pierre de Massot, was 31 years younger than he.

Mother Cocteau paid for his *garçonnière*, his bachelor digs, so luxurious that even his rich friends were impressed. A key to his success was that he didn't limit himself to the acquaintance of beautiful boys, but opened his *salon* to both sexes, young as well as old, although of course there had to be a reason for their presence, at least those who were not physically pleasing and available. Often the sons of Parisian greats were his companions, Lucien Daudet, son of Alphonse Daudet, and Maurice Rostand, son of the truly immense Edmond Rostand, author of *Cyrano de Bergerac*. Thanks to these various contacts he met someone who presented him to Serge Diaghilev (11) and his artistic and homosexual entourage. He encountered the wealthy and hugely connected Anna de Noailles, a woman Cocteau apparently satisfied sexually. He met Proust, but later confided to his mother that Proust's Albertine ''is false. It's a boy!'', which made Proust shameful in Cocteau's eyes because he camouflaged his homosexuality, and it's true that for some of us Proust's work would have been a true masterpiece had he not disguised his male characters as women [which, throughout all his life, he denied doing].

Playwright Robert de Fiers, Proust and Lucien Daudet on the right. Lucien Daudet became a writer and painter, but he is especially known for his friendship with Proust and Cocteau. One of Cocteau's friends, Jean Lorrain, revealed Proust's sexual affair with Lucien, over which Lorrain and Proust fought a duel in 1897. Two shots were exchanged, no one hurt.

Cocteau and Lucien Daudet went to Algiers, the Mecca of boys begging for a few *sous*. He later became friends with Gide who appreciated Cocteau's conversation and social ease, but couldn't digest his mundanity, and the more Cocteau told him his ass smelled like roses, as Cocteau did everyone he judged important enough to frequent, the more Gide disdained his evident lack of sincerity.

Lucien Daudet, 1878-1946, was a writer who lived under the shadow of his famous father. He learned painting under the instruction of Whistler, whom Lucien candidly admitted had taught him to "have great contempt for that which was not first rank, the reason I have contempt for what I do." Jean-Yves Tadié, a French writer and specialist in Proust, wrote that Lucien was "very beautiful, very elegant, a thin and frail young man with a tender and somewhat effeminate face." Writer Jules Renard described Lucien as being "*un beau jeune garçon frisé, lingé, pommadé, peint et poudré*", "A handsome young boy, curly-haired, well-dressed, perfumed, made-up and powdered."

Cocteau met Erik Satie and Picasso and convinced both to put on a ballet, music by Satie, decors by Picasso and choral text by Cocteau, the whole under the direction of Diaghilev. The three went to Rome where Diaghilev was at work, aided by the boy who had replaced his lover Nijinsky, Léonide Massine (11). The result of the collaboration was *Parade*, although

Cocteau's text was dropped. *Parade* had its premiere at the Châtelet Theater in 1917.

Belle Époque art, Leon Bakst's *l'Après-midi d'un faune.*

Cocteau was present at the premiere of Stravinsky's entirely innovative *Sacre du printemps,* which caused a riot and actual fistfights. Cocteau's intelligence, inquisitiveness and charm were such that throughout his life he knew literally everyone worth knowing, and many who weren't, and the reputation of the wildly popular bar Le Boeuf sur le Toit in the early '20s was due largely to Cocteau's presence. Milhaud, Picasso, Diaghilev, Maurice Chevalier, Stravinsky, Poulenc, Satie and Cocteau drew in others, and Cocteau's lover Maurice Sachs chose it as the subject of his book *Au temps de boeuf sur le toit*, 1939. Thoroughly homosexual, it was in the Boeuf that German diplomat Ernst von Rath met and mated with a young Jew, Herschel Grynszpan, who later killed Rath during a lover's quarrel, although the Germans maintained that

Rath was killed for political reasons, an excuse for their launching the Kristallnacht in 1938. [The destiny of Herschel Grynszpan is one of the most fascinating in history. Extremely poor, he left Germany for Paris where, according to the Nazi version, he decided to kill a Nazi in order to avenge 12,000 Polish Germans expelled from Germany to Poland in 1938. He went to the German Embassy where he said he had secret information, and was shown into von Rath's office where he pulled out a gun and shot him. While awaiting trial in Paris his lawyer thought up the homosexual theory as a good defense. When war broke out Herschel was dispatched to Germany where Hitler himself wanted the trial put off when he learned that Herschel was planning to accuse Rath of having been his lover. The last trace of Herschel was his imprisonment up to 1942, after which he simply disappeared. Many historians believe he was executed, others that he wasted away in prison, still others that he lived out the war and spent the remainder of his life back in Paris. Herschel's mother, a death-camp escapee, appeared at Eichmann's 1961 trial to testify against him. The Wikipedia article entitled *Herschel Grynszpan* is a must-read.]

Herschel Grynszpan and von Rath

Cocteau met Raymond Radiguet at a homage to Apollinaire. The 15-year-old was "wrapped up in a beaver coat in which he seemed to have slept. Radiguet cut his way through the crowd where in a muffled voice he read poems, without taking his eyes from the paper, and left alone, like a sleepwalker," wrote Cocteau. Cocteau got him exempted from military service and got his *Le Diable au corps* published by Grasset--today France's first publishing house, the story of an adulterous relationship between a married woman and a young man. Radiguet's next book, *Le bal du comte d'Orgel,* was said to have been written with four hands, his and Cocteau's. Cocteau was Radiguet's Pygmalion, as Gide had been Marc Allégret's. It was said that Cocteau nurtured Radiguet's life with mythology and the heroes of Ancient Greece, all of whom died at the height of their physical and intellectual force, thereby escaping demeaning old age. Some believe that the death of Radiguet, at age 20 from typhus, pushed Cocteau to opium addiction, although Cocteau himself maintained that the two coming at the same time was coincidental. In a 1929 book Cocteau explained how he overcame his addiction, and how during the withdrawal he wrote his most noted play, *Les Enfants terribles*.

Raymond Radiguet

Radiguet went to the Lycée Charlemagne in Paris and decided to launch himself into journalism, working for the *Canard enchaîné*, one of France's most prestigious and iconoclastic weekly newspapers. Bernard Grasset brought out *Le Diable au corps*, as said, in 1923, two years after Cocteau had met Radiguet and had taken him away from Paris where they could write and live among a set of Cocteau's intimates. Grasset's publicity centered around the boy being only 17, which earned laughs from Parisian literati until they read the book and discovered Radiguet's style.

When Radiguet came down with typhus he told Cocteau that he would ''be 'shot in three days by the angels of God'. As I tried to hold back my tears I invented contrary news. 'Your news comes too late,' he said, 'The order has been given. I've heard the order.'

Later he said, 'There's a color circulating and people are hiding in it.' I asked him if he wanted me to chase the people away. 'You can't because you can't see the color.' "

Cocteau then met Jean Desbordes, 1906-1944, a boy who had passed his *baccalauréat*. He became Cocteau's secretary and lover for seven years, beginning in 1926. During the resistance he was known as Duroc and aided in furnishing information that paved the way for the 1944 invasion of Normandy. Caught by the Gestapo, he died under torture. His name is engraved in the Paris Panthéon, resting place of France's greatest heroes.

Jean Desbordes in Cocteau's 1930 film *Le sang d'un Poète.*

When asked why he drugged himself Cocteau answered, "Everything one does in life, even making love, one does it on a train, destination death. Smoking opium is disembarking from that train." Desbordes, besides following Cocteau in his morphine binges, was addicted to gambling along the Riviera, Monte Carlo, Menton and Nice. He would suddenly disappear for periods of time, indifferently with men or woman, all of which pushed Cocteau back to smoking opium, a habit he'd dropped after detoxification.

Desbordes worked on his book *J'adore*, while Cocteau worked on his *Livre blanc* that came out in 1928 in a limited edition of 31 copies. In 1930 Cocteau was asked if the book was by him. He said he'd never admit such an eventuality because people would take it as a kind of autobiography, and that ''I reserve the right to write my own, which will be far more *singulier*'', a French word meaning both strange and remarkable. Gide had published his homosexual book *Corydon* in 1911 and Proust his *Sodom and Gomorrah* in 1921. Cocteau was also at work on a book of drawings showing Desbordes asleep, *25 Drawings of a Sleeper*.

Desbordes

Cocteau's *La Voix humaine* was written with Desbordes in mind. The play has a woman on stage talking to her departing lover, by telephone, trying to convince him that it's not his fault he's leaving her. It ends with her breakdown, pleading with him to hang up. First interpreted by Berthe Bovy [whom Cocteau compared, deservedly, to a Stradivarius], the sound track can be purchased today, a *chef d'oeuvre*. The play has since been translated into numerous languages, interpreted by actors of renown like Ingrid Bergman and Anna Magnani. Those who knew Cocteau knew that the person on the other side of the line was Jean Desbordes, with whom Cocteau was having problems. [If you understand French, you must procure a copy, not forgetting that in reality two men are talking to each other.]

Marcel Khill, age 28, followed Desbordes, whom Cocteau offered a Citroën, at the time an incredibly expensive toy. Henry Gidel, in his *Cocteau*, recounts a little-known story of Cocteau and Khill. Both came across a former boxer in a cabaret, Al Brown, who had lost his world title, a man now heavily dependent on drugs. Incredibly, Cocteau and Krill, thanks to funding by Coco Chanel, got him into shape, and four years after losing his title he won it back in a fight in the Paris Palais des Sports, in front of spectators such as Raimu, Jean Gabin and Tino Rossi. As written in the first line of this chapter, Cocteau was indeed a *touche-à-tout*, a man who had his fingers in absolutely every pie.

Marcel Khill

Khill [Mustapha Marcel Khelilou Ben Abdelkader], 1912-1940, began his career as the lover of the opium addict Maurice Tranchant de Lunel, architect and writer, several times arrested for debauching minors and drug use. Khill was taken in at age 16 and aided Tranchant in organizing orgies, especially those that put young sailors in the hands of officers and high civil servants. Cocteau made little secret of the *"bel avantage arabe"* [well-hung Arab], and Henry Wibbels [one of Marcel Sachs lovers] wrote that Cocteau occasionally liked his sex rough, and once Khill broke three of Cocteau's ribs: *"C'est une brute, mais je l'ai dans la peau"*, [''He's brutal, but I can't do without him''].

Cocteau was stimulated by sailors as well as Arabs, and wrote that ''men from all over the world who love masculine beauty came [to the naval base at Toulon] to admire the sailors who hung out along the docks, alone or in groups, and responded to winks with a smile and never refused the offer of love'', although Cocteau forgot to add: for money. *"De tous les coins du monde, les hommes épris de beauté masculine viennent admirer les marins qui flânent seuls ou par groupes, répondent aux oeillades par un sourire et ne refusent jamais l'offre d'amour."*

For publicity reasons Cocteau decided to relive Jules Verne's *Around the World in 80 Days*, sponsored by the newspaper *Paris-Soir*. He and Khill set off on 28 March 1936 and arrived back in Le Havre on 17 June of the same year. Relations between Cocteau and Khill became strained and Khill decided to join the army, where he died in battle.

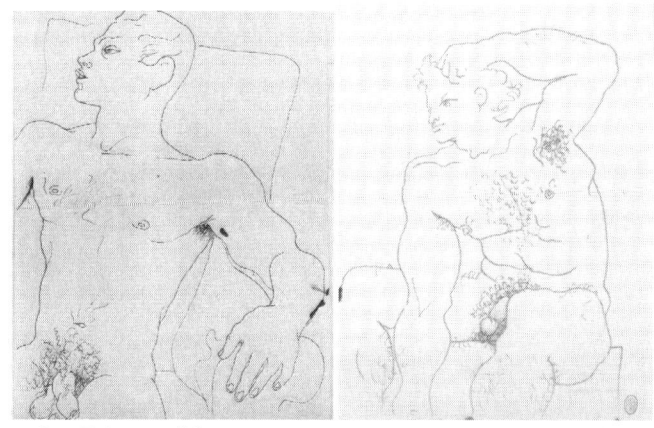

Cocteau's *Livre blanc* came out around this time, in honor of Pierre Dargelos, a boy who benefited from huge prestige thanks to his virility, far above that of those of his age, presumably meaning the size of his phallus and his ability to use it, the subject of the drawings. Some sketches may also be of Marcel Servais, a tattoo-chested sailor called Pas de Chance because he had been down on his luck, a boy whom both Cocteau and Khill shared. Written in 1927, it came out in 1928 under the copyright of Maurice Sachs and Jacques Bonjean [who founded a publishing house together], both of whom falsely claimed they didn't know the identity of the author.**

"*Un des élèves, nommé Dargelos, jouissait d'un grand prestige à cause d'une virilité très au-dessus de son âge. Il s'exhibait avec cynisme et faisait commerce d'un spectacle qu'il donnait même à des élèves d'une autre classe en échange de timbres rare ou de tabac*". ["**One of the students, Dargelos, was hugely favored because he was virile far beyond his age, and would cynically exhibit himself, even to students from other classes, in exchange for rare stamps or tobacco.**"]

One of Cocteau's first memories was seeing ''two boys, naked, climb a tree, their tanned bodies enhanced by three black regions'' [head hair, underarms and pubis]. ''If I live a hundred years I'll never forget,'' he wrote much later. Cocteau's family had a servant, Gustave, and after seeing the two naked boys Cocteau decided he wanted to touch the places that had so aroused his imagination, especially as the servant had a large bulge in his trousers. Cocteau drew a naked woman that he showed the servant and when Cocteau saw he was excited he reached out and caressed the extended tissue. The servant's reaction was to go red and pinch Cocteau's ear, but deathly afraid of losing his place, ''*mort de peur de perdre sa place*'', he simply showed Cocteau out of the room.

Les Enfants terribles was filmed starring Jean Marais. It's a story so twisted that it couldn't have been invented, and indeed it was inspired by the lives of two of Cocteau's friends, his intimate buddy Jean Bourgoint [1905-1966] and Jean's sister Jeanne. *How* "intimate" Jean was with Cocteau is not known, but Jeanne followed Cocteau into opium addiction, and committed suicide at age 20 [an occurance common at the time, especially in the Bloomsbury Set (16)]. Brother and sister both lived a dissipated life alongside Cocteau, their haven Le Boeuf sur la Toit. At the death of his sister Jean entered the orders and finished his life a monk in a leper-clinic in Cameroun.

In Cocteau's play Jean is Paul and Jeanne, Elizabeth. At their mother's death they invent a game, used to push each other into doing exploits, for example stealing, and to see who could more successfully hurt the other's feelings, the winner being he or she who had the last word. They make outside acquaintances along the way, a certain Delgado that Paul loves and who injures Paul when he throws a snowball at him with a rock inside. There is also Agatha, who physically resembles Delgado, and thereby attracts Paul.

Elizabeth decides to anger Paul by marrying a young man, who dies just after the ceremony but before the honeymoon and sexual felicity with Elizabeth. Elizabeth inherits his home where she and Paul install themselves.

Because part of the game is to hurt the other, when Elizabeth sees that Paul is interested in Agatha, the Delgado lookalike, she introduces her to Gerard whom Elizabeth bullies into marrying Agatha, which breaks Paul's heart.

In the meantime Delgado has become a collector of poisons, one of which he sends Paul. Having lost Agatha, Paul takes the poison after writing a letter to Agatha declaring his love for her. Agatha, who has only really loved Paul, something she had confided to

Elizabeth, came running to Paul's side and they realize that it had been Elizabeth who had suborned their love. When Elizabeth learned that Paul was on his deathbed, and in dying it would be he who had the last word, she hurriedly shot herself, seconds before his last breath.

Jean-Marais' early life centered around Jean Cocteau, a man 20 years older who could do--and did do--everything to advance Marais' career, in the way that Gide did for Marc Allégret. While Gide and Marc at times included others in their sexual relations, such encounters were routine between Cocteau and Marais, Cocteau who attracted hordes of boys thanks to his contacts, charm and intelligence, boys who turned to Marais to fulfill their lust, but slept with Cocteau to advance their careers, and Marais who attracted boys thanks to his beauty, boys Cocteau would benefit from as he had benefited from Marc Allégret when presented to him by Gide. An example of this was Cocteau's encounter with Denham Fouts, the best-kept prostitute of the times, as seen in this extract from my book *American Homosexual Giants*: ''Stephen Spender dropped in during Denny's absence and his and Peter's relationship began anew. Denny returned to Paris in '38 while Peter was on a trip abroad with Spender and, one night, doped, he decided to see Jean Marais, Cocteau's lover, who was acting in Cocteau's *Les Parents terribles*. He went to the theater in pajamas and insisted on seeing Cocteau who, when he got a look at the beautiful Denny said, *'Mais naturellement. La pièce était écrite pour être vue en pyjama!'* '' [''The play was *written* to be seen in pajamas'']. We don't know if Cocteau had Denny, but Marais did.

It was the ultimate symbiosis, with a major difference for the times in that the relationship took place even during the war, when any of Hitler's henchmen could have had both sent to concentration camps, a pink triangle on their coats, and no one would have been able to do anything to save either.

Cocteau was clearly in love with Marais [whom he called ''the people's Antinous''], and he sent him this letter in 1939, around five years after they'd met, Marais away serving in the French forces under Leclerc: ''I know now the sickness I'm suffering from: you. Living without you. I look for you like a poor blind dog. I lie down and then get back up and look for you elsewhere. Life without you is atrocious.'' [''*Je sais maintenant le mal dont je souffre et que je traîne : c'est toi. C'est vivre sans toi. Je te cherche partout comme un pauvre chien aveugle et je me couche pour une minute. Je me lève et je te cherche ailleurs. Vivre sans toi est atroce.*'']

Marais never let Cocteau's desire for him limit his desire for others, and over the years, as he became a popular actor, making 100 films in which he did his own stunts, he gradually freed himself from Cocteau's hold, becoming more a friend, a respectful son, and even Cocteau's protector. ''My quest has always been happiness,'' Marais wrote, ''and I've always done what was needed to fulfill that happiness, even when it meant lying in order to please.'' [''*Le bonheur a toujours été un don chez moi. J'ai toujours fait ce qu'il fallait pour être heureux. J'ai même appris à mentir pour plaire.*'']

Jean Alfred Villain-Marais was born in Cherbourg in 1913, a picturesque town, the port of entry for those coming to France by ship, as I did on the *Queen Mary*.

Marais' veterinarian father left the house when Marais was around age 4 and his mother took him and his brother to Paris. He stayed with his aunt because his mother was often absent. Only later did he learn that she, a kleptomaniac, was regularly away in prison, when not elsewhere with one of her lovers. Perhaps because she'd lost a daughter, she put Jean in girl's clothes and curled his hair. He was expelled from school when he arrived dressed as a girl to please a professor who was then courting him.

Marais, Cocteau and Marais.

When one failed to enter the Conservatoire, as was Marais' case, one took private classes offered by theater and film directors, and in 1937 Marais paid to be admitted into the classes of the renowned Charles Dullin. During tryouts for Cocteau's *Oedipe Roi*, Cocteau saw and fell in love with him. This first meeting, in 1937, was followed by Marais' role in Cocteau's *Les Parents terrible* in 1938. He starred in *La Belle et la Bête* [1946], a film that had been extremely difficult due to hours of make-up, special effects and the sentiment that a film so inventive would be a flop. Instead, it made both Cocteau and Marais famous throughout France [a film Marais made with his wife of two years, Mila Parély]. Marais starred in *L'Aigle à deux têtes* in 1949 and then *Orphée*. He later got his revenge for having been turned away by the Conservatoire by entering the ultra-prestigious Comédie-Française.

Les Parents terribles is the story of middle-aged George who has a mistress, Madeleine. His wife Yvonne is ill, and her sister Léo, an old maid, is in love with George. The couple has a son, Michel, who wants to introduce his parents to a girl he likes, Madeleine, his father's mistress. George threatens to tell his son all if Madeleine continues to see his boy. Michel is inconsolable when Madeleine leaves him but Léo persuades George and Yvonne to allow him to marry the girl, after which Léo commits suicide.

In *Orphée* Jean Marais is a famous poet who meets with a Princess and Cégeste [Cocteau's lover and adopted son Édouard Dermit], a handsome young poet, in the Café des Poètes. Drunk, Cégeste starts a brawl. The police are called and Cégeste, in trying to escape arrest, flees the café and is run down by two motorcyclists. The Princess has his body put in her car and heads for her chateau, accompanied by Orpheus and the two motorcyclists.

Dermit and Cocteau.

At the chateau the Princess brings Cégeste back to life and he, she and the two motorcyclists disappear into a mirror, leaving Orpheus alone. Orpheus is taken home by the Princess's chauffeur. There he joins his wife who is soon killed by the two motorcyclists, sent to do the killing by the Princess who is in reality Death. The chauffeur tells Orpheus he'll take him to her, through the mirror. In the Underworld a tribunal decides that Orpheus' wife was unjustly killed, and that she could return home on the condition that Orpheus never again look at her. He agrees and it is under these conditions that one day, while Orpheus is repairing a car, he inadvertently sees his wife through the car rearview mirror, and she vanishes.

Orpheus returns to the café where a group of people, believing him responsible for Cégeste's death, attack and kill him. He descends to the Underworld where a new tribunal declares both his and his wife's death illegal, and so both are sent to the world of the living, their memories of the previous events erased.

During the occupation Cocteau steered a middle course between what was acceptable and what was not, under the Germans. Jean Marais played to huge crowds at the Comédie-Française, and afterwards he and Cocteau went to the best restaurants and the finest cabarets. Both were invited to an exposition of German Arno Breker's sculptures in the Orangerie on the grounds of the Louvre, naked males exactly as Cocteau and Marais liked them. Cocteau wrote an article that would later haunt him, in which he saluted Breker as a second Michelangelo, ''whose *David* has shown you [Breker] the way'' [''*la grande main de* David *de Michel-Ange vous a montré votre route.*''], while nearby Jean Desbordes and Jean Moulin were soon to be tortured to death, along with many, many others. Cocteau later claimed that Breker had used his influence to save him from being shipped off to a concentration camp, Breker ''*qui m'a sauvé de pire... Je ne l'oublierai jamais*'' [''who saved me from the worst... I'll never forget him''].

Breker's art.

Whatever the accusations, men like Cocteau and

Sasha Guitry [sent to jail for collaborating with the Germans], were masters in the art of verbal self-defense. In Cocteau's case he wrote that the BBC accused him of cooperating with the enemy, while the German Nazis stated he was a Gaullist. Near the end of the war Jean Marais left to join the forces of French General Leclerc.

In 1946, while visiting friends, Cocteau was introduced to an Italian, age 22, a mineworker who painted in his spare time. Cocteau engaged him as his gardener, stating, "I can't help every miner in the world, but I will help him." The new boy was Édouard Dermit [who later played in the above *Orphée*]. Jean Marais was most probably pleased; young, popular and rich, for him the world was still his oyster, and he was now free from the constraints imposed by his former lover. How much sex was involved between Dermit and Cocteau will never be known, although by then Cocteau claimed: "As far as sex is concerned ... I now live the life of a monk." [Which didn't stop him, even in old age, from having several liftings and hair transplants, and when filmed he covered bald stops with cigar ash.]

It was during the '50s that Marais left the gravitational pull of Cocteau, making films with Visconti, Renoir, Sacha Guitry and Bertolucci. He then left Cocteau definitively for the American dancer George Reich.

George Reich

The remainder of Cocteau's life was made up of expositions of his paintings, tapestries and drawings; film homages; inaugurations; miscellaneous honors; and voyages with Dermit. He suffered several heart attacks, a final one opening the perspective of still another adventure, this one for all eternity.

Dermit, also a painter, was with Cocteau on every voyage, right to the end.

In the 1960s Marais adopted a boy, Serge Ayala,

whom he later claimed was his son. Serge later took the name Serge Villain-Marais. Marais had known Serge's mother during the war, and brought the boy to live with him and Cocteau in Marne-la-Coquette. Marais employed him in his films but Serge had his own character and, as would happen between Alain Delon his son Anthony, there were epic disagreements and separations. At his death Marais left Serge nothing, and only following years of legal battles did Serge come into Marais' money [under French law parents are *obliged* to leave part of their wealth to their children]. By then he lived alone, with four dogs, stating that his ambition, now that he had funds, was to find a wife and found a family. Instead he committed suicide in 2012.

Marais did mostly stage work until he was in his eighties. He had always been a sculptor and in 1989 he created his *Le Passe Muraille* in Montmartre. He wrote his *Mémoires* and *L'Inconcevable Jean Cocteau*.

Le Passe Muraille

Jean Marais died in Cannes in 1998.

André Gide

Gide and Cellini had a point in common, a father who desired a son with all his heart, loving and playful as a man must best be with his boy, but in Gide's case his luck ended with his father's early death, leaving him in the hands of his disciplinarian mother and her female companion, who fought to break his curiosity and enthusiasm and bring him into the fold of the conformist majority. This was not auspicious soil to bring up a child, and although he would break the mold, the joy for life gave way to a saturnine search for fulfillment in his art and in his sex life, a sexuality that would make him doubt that *love* had anything to do with natural lust, the wondrous body of a lad being in itself enough, both who would mutually ejaculate before wandering off, each content, each ready for adventures elsewhere [which doesn't mean that the sex hadn't been without romanticism]. Today we're used to saunas, baths, backrooms and dark alleys where lust alone suffices, but in Gide's time love was expected to be an integral part of the sexual experience, making Gide a Roaring Twenties precursor in fleeting carnal couplings.

Gide, young. Gide was uncontestably the Roaring Twenties' major writer.

Because he was good at school, because he had an educated accent, school boys laid in wait for him and beat him up: "There were days when I got home in a terrible state, my clothes all torn and muddied, my nose bleeding, my teeth chattering, distraught with fear," a quote brought to us by Alan Sheridan in his definitive *André Gide*, 1998.

The breakthrough to sexual liberation would not come easily, where everything was a sin and all pleasure had to be hidden under his blankets [Gide became an enthusiastic masturbator, outside of sex as well as during and immediately after sex, as a solitary prolongation of the afterglow, reliving the boy's body in his mind]. Sex was to be secret, although he wrote a defense of homosexuality in 1920, *Corydon*, but only at the advanced age of 51--yet he nonetheless did put it on paper, a rarity then.

Gide, never satisfied with less than six orgasms in a row.

Gide married his cousin, a girl he had known all his life, his deepest and closest friend throughout his adolescence, a religiously pious girl who had had her own problems, difficulties that united them as two survivors on a hostile planet, taking comfort in their exchange of whispered confidences. "Drugged with love ... and pity, I called on God with all my strength and offered myself, no longer able to imagine any other aim than to protect that child against fear, against evil, against life," wrote Gide in his *La Porte étroite* [*Straight is the Gate*]. "It was as if there was nothing good inside me that did not come from her. My childish love became indistinguishable from my religious fervor. It seemed to me that, as I drew nearer to God, I came closer to her." When Madeleine's mother ran off with a lover, she took refuge in religion, spending the rest of her life in virtuous retreat, sparing Gide any sexual obligation in a marriage that would never be consumed [as I've said elsewhere in this book, this kind of marriage, commonplace especially in England at the time, is unthinkable today, except when one is obliged to hide one's homosexuality as do, for example, actors and politicians].

His first novel was *Les Cahiers d'André Walter*, which told of his courting Madeleine and the opposition of his mother to his marriage, his mother's death followed by Madeleine's. This was in 1891. In 1892 he crossed the path of Oscar Wilde.

Gide and the author of the recently published *The Picture of Dorian Gray* met and, according to Wilde, it was he who introduced Gide to the "love that dare not speak its name", a phrase coined by Wilde's lover Alfred Douglas, although Gide later maintained that he had had homosexual experiences before meeting Wilde. Both men ventured to Tunisia where Wilde offered to procure Gide's first Arab boy for him. In a strangled voice Gide agreed, giving way to the most exciting experience of Gide's life: "Wilde took a key out of his pocket and showed me into a tiny apartment of two rooms.... The youths followed him, each of them wrapped in a burnoose that hid his face. Then the guide left us and Wilde sent me into the further room with little Mohammed and shut himself up in the other with the [other boy]. Every time since then that I have sought after pleasure, it is the memory of that night I have pursued.... My joy was unbounded, and I cannot imagine it greater, even if love had been added.

"How should there have been any question of love? How should I have allowed desire to dispose of my heart? No scruple clouded my pleasure and no remorse followed it. But what name then am I to give the rapture I felt as I clasped in my naked arms that perfect little body, so wild, so ardent, so somberly lascivious? For a long time after Mohammed's departure I remained in a state of passionate jubilation, and though I had already achieved pleasure five times with him, I renewed my ecstasy again and again, and when I got back to my room in the hotel, I prolonged its echoes until morning.''

Gide explained to his friend Martin du Gard that he nearly always needed to ejaculate six or seven times consecutively. He would come twice in rapid succession, to the surprise of his partners, and then a third time. After the partner left he would come again, preferably with someone else but if not he would jerk off three or more times before he felt satisfied.

His mother died, and Gide's reaction was startlingly honest: ''I felt dazed, like a prisoner suddenly set free, like a kite whose string has suddenly been cut, like a boat broken loose from its moorings, like a drifting wreck, at the mercy of wind and tides.'' It was immediately afterwards that he married Madeleine. Gide was happy to note that unlike men, Madeleine hadn't an iota of lust, and had even told Gide that she had a mental terror ''of sex''. Gide was thusly free to travel to North Africa, to haunt the urinals on the Continent and to go to the baths, often accompanied by friends as randy as he. He took up photography, a way of procuring Italian models, boys more restrained than Arabs, reminiscent of Gore Vidal, years later, who would drive up to a group of Italian lads in his convertible, around which they would enthusiastically gather, and while they inspected it he would choose the best-looking and tell him, ''You're the most beautiful boy I've ever seen'', and see what went down from there--although *always* in exchange for money (23).

Gide found love in the arms of Marc Allégret, the love of his life, age 15 to Gide's 48. Gide had known Marc's father, a pastor who had helped Gide get through the oppressive years of his youth, and in thanks he fucked his son, in one of life's stranger charades [in Ancient Greece the men a father had to watch most carefully in the protection of his son's anal virginity were the father's closest friends and male family members (17)]. Gide went to London with the boy, abandoning Madeleine who sought revenge by burning his letters, some of the thousands Gide would write throughout his life, all of which were of dire importance to him. ''For a whole week I wept without stopping,'' he later wrote, his wife apparently believing that the pain would pull her husband closer to God, and away from his sins. At any rate his love of Marc inspired his book *The Counterfeiters, Les Faux-monnayeurs*, the story of Marc and their love, one of the books of Gide's *oeuvre* still read.

Gide and Marc

During his relationship with Marc, Gide sired a daughter, which greatly disturbed Marc and was a key factor in their later separation [although during most of their years together Marc, bisexual, never hesitated to go as far as girls allowed him to go].

When he published *Cordon* he lost many friends, even some homosexual friends who didn't like Gide's disdain for homosexual love that didn't follow the purity of Hellenic relationships. Heterosexuals naturally spurned him because of his treatment of Madeleine [and ingrained homophobia]. In revenge, he put his personal library up for auction, books dedicated to him by the literary giants of the time, stating exactly why he was doing so in the auction catalogue, which had to be rewritten by the director of sales to omit that precision. But like *Corydon* itself, it was an example of Gide who always sought to be honest, with himself first, with others afterwards, no matter how honest he was in reality.

Corydon was a Greek shepherd, as we see in this extract from my book *Mediterranean Homosexual Pleasure*:

Corydon the shepherd burned with love for the handsome Alexis. Alone, with unquenched passion, he flung his words to the woods and hills: ''Oh cruel Alexis, so you care nothing for my songs? Have you no pity for me? You'll force me to die at last. Was it not better to endure Amaryllis' sullen anger, and scornful pride? Or Menalcas, though he was dark and you are blond? I'm scorned by you, Alexis: you don't ask who I am, how rich in cattle, how overflowing with snowy milk. A thousand of my lambs wander Sicilian hills, fresh milk does not fail me, in summer or in winter. I'm not so hideous: I saw myself the other day on the shore when the sea was calm without a breeze, if the mirror never lies. If you'd only live with me in the lowly countryside, in a humble cottage, shooting deer and driving the flocks of kids. I keep the kids for you even though Thestylis has long begged to take them from me. And she probably shall, since my gifts seem worthless to you. O lovely boy, come here: see what the Nymphs bring for you, lilies in heaped baskets, pale violets and heads of poppy flowers for you. Narcissi with fragrant fennel flowers for you. I'll gather fruit, pale with soft down and chestnuts to which I'll add waxy plums: they too shall be for you. I'll pluck laurels and myrtle so when placed next to you you will mingle your sweet perfumes. Oh Corydon, you're so foolish: Alexis cares nothing for gifts, nor if you fought with gifts would Iollas yield. The fierce lioness hunts the wolf, the wolf hunts the goat, the wanton goat hunts for flowering clover. O Alexis, Corydon hunts you and I hunt him: each is led by his passion. Love burns me, for what limits has love?'' End of extract.

Corydon was a name often used by poets to designate shepherds. As for Gide's book, the central idea is that love between males flourished in Ancient Greece (31), Ancient Rome (35), Renaissance Italy (8) and Elizabethan England [and especially Victorian England (10)], an apparently new concept at the time. The small book was translated into many languages and sold thousands of copies [perhaps because the buyer thought it would be homoerotic, which is not the case].

Gide by Paul Albert Laurens.

Alan Sheridan asks the reasonable question, What did 15-year-old Marc Allégret see in 48-year-old André Gide. Certainly André awoke the boy intellectually and sexually, like Socrates ''teaching his young lover how to use his body as well as his mind,'' writes Sheridan. Early on in the relationship André had promised Marc that he would ''initiate the young man into heterosexuality'', continued Sheridan. Marc had made a few attempts at seducing girls, and after one failure he had been devastated and ''retired to his bedroom and sobbed his heart out''.

Marc Allégret.
Marc easily accepted Gide's love and Gide promised to initiate him in heterosexual intercourse, as would a father or an uncle at the time, by sending the lad to a prostitute.

For Marc, André was an ideal mentor, possessing immense intellect, and he led the envious life of a world traveler, when seen through the eyes of a schoolboy. Marc seems to have entered into the physical aspects without the slightest reticence or shame, as though he felt it was a normal step from boyhood to manhood. Later, Marc would become a film director, would marry at age 37 and have a daughter, as well as mistresses along the way. Gide stated that he had never felt jealousy towards his other lovers, but Marc was the exception. A remarkably similar case took place between Christopher Isherwood and his very young lover, Don Bachardy, whom Isherwood literally raised to adulthood, paying for his education, sending him off to England to the best schools of art, and, later, helped him to choose boys who were young and beautiful, although, Isherwood being Isherwood, he would also often profit from threesomes consisting of Don, a new youth and himself (23).

Gide hit the nail on the head when he wrote,

"Marc loves me not so much for what I am as for what I enable him to be."

Gide went off to Cambridge with Marc [as Isherwood would do with Bachardy] where his age, in comparison to the "glorious body of Marc" and the students rowing on the Thames, was difficult for him to digest. He met the members of the Bloomsbury Set, the *nec plus ultra* of the homosexual upper-crust of the times (16).

Marc was André's Fountain of Youth. "He is my adolescence; without him I would be my age. One must refresh oneself in the company of the young if one is to keep going on." Gide had introduced Marc to Cocteau and became deathly afraid that Cocteau's charm and worldliness would seduce the boy, which he did. Cocteau later wrote that he knew that Gide would have killed him if he could have, even if, publicly and in their correspondence, both remained two-faced friends. Cocteau introduced Marc into the world of the theater and presented him to the many boys that gravitated around Cocteau and were bedded by both Cocteau and his lover Jean Marais, one of whom was the American writer Gore Vidal (23).

In 1927 Marc and André went on a trip to the Congo during which Marc had sexual experiences with Congolese women, which favored his heterosexual initiation. His sexual break with Gide is thought to have dated from then. Marc's first experience, at least with African women, took place when he was joined by a girl during his siesta, and from then on, for a pittance, he could offer himself whomever he wished, the average age being 14. As for Gide, he went with boys, stating, "It happened so naturally, so easily," [a quote from Sheridan]. Even in black Africa Gide usually had Arab boys, one of whom he'd met in Brazzaville and traveled with him for seven months. Both the boy, Adoum, and Gide tried to hold back their tears on parting: "I have never seen anything more moving than that poor boy's unhappiness," wrote Gide. During the journey Marc took hundreds of meters of film, the beginning of his life-long career, Marc then 21, André 56.

Marc Allégret went on to direct more than 50 films, an enormous output, as well as writing many of the scripts. Among his discoveries were Michèle Morgan, Jean-Paul Belmondo, Raimu [perhaps France's greatest actor], the beloved Gérard Philipe, Louis Jourdan, Jean-Louis Barrault, as well as making films with Alain Delon and Patrick Dewaere, who was an amazing cinematographic presence until his suicide.

Roger Martin du Gard had discovered Berlin and its total sexual liberty, "The beauty of the young people, the simplicity of their morals ... prostitution of both sexes ... sexual relations, at once light-hearted, serious and free, without flirting or vulgarity. Pornography too is everywhere and delighted in, without shame of hypocrisy." [The full story of sexuality during this time can be found in my book *German Homosexuality*.] Roger Martin du Gard convinced Gide and Marc to join him there. Marc soon returned to Paris [we don't know what he did sexually in Berlin] and Gide went to North Africa where he discovered Fez, a place Roger Martin du Gard said was necessary to visit for a few days every fortnight, "to purge one's mind and body".

The plot of Gide's *Faux-Monnayeurs* is not easy to summarize because it interweaves several different plots, many characters, a number of whom are homosexual and bisexual, men as counterfeit as the counterfeit gold coins of the story. Gide presumably called on his memory concerning a number of school chums when writing the book, and himself is the benevolent Édouard who is pitted against the malevolent Comte de Passavent, most likely Jean Cocteau.

Gide was never a card-carrying communist but believed in its potentiality for social good [''It is a promise of salvation for mankind''] until he visited the U.S.S.R. in 1936, about which he wrote an essay in *The God That Failed*.

He won the Nobel Prize for Literature in 1947 and was the first living artist published in the prestigious *Pléiade*.

In 1939 Gide went to Luxor where he wrote that the boys were not only available, but in competition with each other for the attention of men like Gide. But ''I no longer have the great wish to fornicate,'' he wrote, now age 70, and so it is here we will leave him. The Fountain of Youth is indeed a fountain reserved for the young, and so the reader is advised to let no new adventure escape him: ''Didn't it go by awfully fast?'' said Gore Vidal's lover of 56 years on his deathbed. Gide himself died old, but his life had certainly gone by just as awfully fast.

Maurice Ravel

In the world of today we have two remaining enigmas, the Loch Ness monster and Ravel's sexuality, both sounded for years, both have their supporters and detractors, both occasionally resolved until a new sighting, a new document surfaces to question everything we thought we knew.

Everything about Ravel, [Joseph Maurice Ravel, 1875-1937], is chiaroscuro contrast. His mother was the love of his life, whose death in 1917 plunged him into ''horrible despair'' she being ''my only reason for living''. He wrote a song, *Sainte*, set to a poem by Stéphane Mallarmé in her honor. She was Basque [the Basque country comprises seven provinces, four in Spain and three in France] and it was in the Basque town of Ciboure that Ravel was born. Said to have been barely literate, she had lived a number of years in Spain and her folk songs, in Basque and Spanish, are said to have had a lasting influence on the masterpieces her son would write. His father was an engineer and invented the Whirlwind of Death, an automobile loup-the-loup adopted by the Barnum and Bailey Circus until it led to a fatal accident in 1913, after which it was abandoned.

Ravel, the leading composer of France's Roaring Twenties.

Chiaroscuro is especially evident in Ravel's private life, where some who knew him insisted he went to whorehouses in search of feminine company because he was too aware of his short stature, 5' 2'', to dare search for sex on his own. His best friend was the young pianist Ricardo Viñes whom at least one very serious biographer maintained was his lover, and that when both, still just boys, lived in Paris, in its sexual center, Pigalle, they would look down from their balcony on a café frequented by artists and their models, and try to determine who was bedding whom, which, if true, says a great deal about a boy, Ravel, who was supposedly interested in nothing other than musical composition. Viñes would later become the teacher of gay composer Francis Poulenc.

Physically, Ravel was of great beauty, and only his height was a psychological handicap, because what counts is proportion, and in that he was perfect, even if the contrast did make his head seem overly big. At age

20 he was, in the words of his biographer Burnett James, "self-possessed, a little aloof ... given to banter." Everyone agrees that he dressed like a dandy. Musicologist Arbie Orenstein wrote that he had the appearance of a well-dressed jockey" [again, due to his small stature]. Ricardo Viñes lovingly wrote that he looked "like a Florentine page, standing straight and stiff, with bangs and flowing black hair."

Others state he seemed to have been satisfied with his physical appearance, as well he should have been, and was clearly the beauty of the family. One biographer said his enchantment with himself developed into time-consuming narcissism. This was certified by Alma Mahler whom she and her husband put up for three weeks: "He came to breakfast rouged and perfumed, in bright satin robes that he loved."

During a certain concert in Chicago he wouldn't perform because his evening shoes had been left at the railway station [the shoes would have not been visible to the audience]. The guest soprano, Lisa Roma, had to take a taxi there to retrieve them, while the spectators and the Chicago Symphony Orchestra waited.

His intelligence was described as sharp and his wit keen when among friends he felt comfortable with, most of whom were intellectual snobs, as Ravel was said to have been.

During W.W. I, at age 40, he became a lorry driver, hauling around munitions that could have come under German bombing. He wrote *Ma mère l'Oye* before the war, found "absolutely ravishing, a masterpiece in miniature" wrote the journal *Mercure de France*, and during the war he wrote *Le tombeau de*

Couperin, dedicated to those who had perished in the conflagration.

Ravel's father knew Erik Satie who was eking out a living as a café pianist. He introduced him to his son who found Satie's work "of inestimable value", as it indeed is, his *Gymnopédies* the proof. Ravel and Satie would eventually have a falling-out, as Ravel would with nearly everyone he had been close to, including Stravinsky. Ravel had been privileged to attend the first performance of *Le Sacre du printemps* and had highly praised it, Stravinsky thanking him, adding that Ravel was the only person capable of understanding it. They then collaborated on several works until Stravinsky wrote *Les Noces* that Ravel said he didn't like, which ended their friendship. Ravel had worked extremely closely with Diaghilev who had commissioned Ravel's wonderful *Daphnis et Chloé*, that Stravinsky said was "one of the most beautiful products of all French music." Then Diaghilev commissioned *La Valse*, but turned it down as "a masterpiece, but it's not a ballet", thusly ending their relationship. [*La Valse* was nonetheless produced as a ballet twice before Diaghilev's death, to Ravel's satisfaction.]

He turned Mussorgsky's *Pictures at an Exhibition* into a masterpiece by reorchestrating it in 1922, after Mussorgsky's death, the original work having generated no interest until then.

He went to America in 1928 and played 25 cities at a guaranteed minimum $10,000. He was fascinated by American dynamism as was Camille Saint-Saëns before him, and praised the quality of American orchestras. He was heart warmed when he found that he had only to show himself before an audience to get a standing ovation, "Something that doesn't happen in Paris," he stated. In New York he met George Gershwin who told him he wanted to become his student. "Why do you want to become a second-rate Ravel when you're already a first-class Gershwin?" asked Ravel. Unlike Americans, the French never discuses money, so it was exceptional for Ravel to ask Gershwin how much he made for his concerts. When Gershwin answered, Ravel said, "Perhaps I should study under Gershwin."

In 1898 he wrote his first work for full orchestra, the magnificent *Shéhérazade*.

Ravel's *Bolero* was written just after the American tour, also in 1928, and is without doubt his most famous composition, commissioned by Ida Rubinstein for her ballet company. It was Maurice Béjart who would immortalize it in his own Ballet du xxe siècle, certain to win him standing ovations each time it was performed. Ravel was astonished at its success, calling it, "seventeen minutes ... of wholly orchestral tissue without music", adding, "there are no contrasts, and there is practically no invention…. Repetition takes the place of development." When told that an elderly lady had shouted out "Rubbish!" when performed the first time, Ravel answered, "That old lady got the message!" Ravel summed up his feelings in a comment to Arthur Honegger, "I've written only one masterpiece--Bolero. Unfortunately there's no music in it!" He limited Bolero to 17 minutes, following the advice of Edgar Allen Poe that a poem can only sustain excitement if under half an hour, the limit Ravel put on most of his works. He used saxophones in his orchestration, a first, and later incorporate jazz in his compositions, another first, and confirmation of how open he was to new sounds, something that had begun as early as the Exposition Universelle in Paris in 1889 when he was struck by the works of Rimsky-Korsakov, there to conduct in person.

The *Concerto pour la main gauche*, first performed in Vienna in 1932, was written at the request of Austrian pianist Paul Wittgenstein who had lost his right arm during the war, a work so difficult to perform that Ravel was obliged to use both his hands. It is truly one of the most beautiful creations written for the human ear.

His final years were cruel, and although what he eventually died of is not precisely known, it may have been Alzheimer's. He passed away at age 62, an atheist, and there was no religious ceremony, as he requested.

Jacques d'Adelswärd-Fersen

During the time of Jacques d'Adelswärd-Fersen [whom I'll call Fersen from here on], rich boys often turned to writing poetry to justify their existence, something Byron did. It is extremely difficult to judge the homosexual allusions in their works because in modern times we need a Rosetta Stone to understand what they were trying to reveal to us. The basis for the obscurity were the laws of the land, so severe that one could be pilloried--caged in public, splattered with shit if one were lucky, one's eyes gouged out or throat pierced if one were not--or hanged by the neck until dead--or both, an excellent reason to encipher one's thoughts and lusts. In comparison, the texts from Ancient Greece, 2000 years earlier, are as clear as sparkling Spartan mountain cascades. Fersen was lucky in that France had given up burning boy-lovers since 1791, following the French Revolution, but one was nonetheless forbidden to incite boys to debauch or to debauch minors. There were also laws against public indecency. The police in Paris used this provision of the law as an excuse to raid taverns, brothels, parks, and other hangouts of sexual adventure. Scandal was an ever-hazardous threat, and nobody, absolutely nobody, wanted to be accused of vile sodomy, especially not when one was a noble, or the head of a family, or the father of children, or the director of a factory or enterprise.

Fersen, the catalyst of Very Bad Things.

In the case of Fersen, as for Byron, his taste for boys dated back to boarding-school dormitories (4), and the remembrance of fresh, young, often virgin bodies, a taste that frequently increased as one aged. While anything was permissible in schools among students, having sex was as illegal then as it is today when adults are involved. In Renaissance Florence boys were bought on the street from age 9, which was also against the law but so prevalent that the adult offender got off with a fine [unless the boy was forced, in which case men could be--and at times were--burned alive].

Born in Paris in 1880, Fersen's grandfather, a Swedish count, founded a steel industry at Longwy in the east of France, which Fersen inherited at age 22, his father having died at age 40, perhaps of yellow fever contracted in Panama, when Fersen was seven. Fersen had a brother, Renold, who died young. Both father and brother were greatly loved by Fersen, if one can judge from the characters in his books, often named Axel after his father, and Renold. Fersen went to Science-Po in Paris, its best school then as today, and the University of Geneva. His literary reputation resides on his *oeuvre*, ten collections of poems, three novels and the creation of a literary review called *Akademos*.

Fersen

His best friend and lover was Hans de Warren, a school chum with whom he would pick up boys, often directly as they left their *lycées*, at times in parks. The lads were invited home to Fersen's wealthy residence near the Arc de Triomphe after a joyride in the family royal-blue Darracq, driven by a liveried chauffeur. There the boys would be offered cakes and wine, shown Fersen and Warren's extensive collection of pornography, and, thus excited, they would be masturbated and blown. There is no record of anal sex, but the subject would have been avoided even by later police investigators, or referred to in such general terms as to make denial easy, to the relief of the offenders and the questioners. One of the boys confessed that Fersen drew a picture of his penis, and he measured that of another, hard. A third lad said that after inhaling ether and ingesting morphine, Fersen, misty-eyed, proposed that they both go to Venice where he would give the boy half his fortune, and where they would die in a suicide pact.

All of this came out after the incident that brought both Fersen and Warren to trial. Both boys, in their early twenties, organized living tableaux that they put on in front of an audience. The actors in the tableaux were all young boys, from age 7 to 17, the average age being 14. The seven-year-old had an extremely early sexual awakening, thanks to his brothers who were participants, and whose talk and nightly masturbation filled him in on adolescent sex. During the tableaux the boys took poses while poetry was read. The boys, as well as the audience, were made up of the crème of Parisian society, the boys coming from the very best families and schools, the audience being formed of men--but some women--estimated as 70% pederastic. During the tableaux one of the boys would always be naked, his privates covered by gauze if seen frontally, his buttock *au naturel* if lying on a couch or the floor. Afterwards they would retire to the bathroom to clean up. Aroused by their performance, they gratefully allowed the two older boys to masturbate and fellate them. Fersen and Warren would also allow themselves to be manipulated until ejaculation.

The séances went on twice a week, Thursdays and Sundays, until the father of the seven-year-old found out and demanded that the police arrest Fersen and Warren, threatening, when they hesitated because of the families involved, to go public if they didn't. They did, but he went public anyway, and the resultant scandal was horrendous. The seven-year-old and his two brothers must have gone through hell at the hand of their daddy, but of this we know nothing.

Fersen was examined by three psychiatrists, one of which purportedly diagnosed him with inherited insanity, alcoholism and epilepsy. A physician, Doctor Socquet, found he had scabies [a contagious skin infection caused by mites] and gonorrhea, and the judge questioning him, as well as his clerk, were said to have gone to public baths after each interrogation to avoid contamination [private bathrooms in one's apartment were still rare at the time].

A fictional account of the tableaux, called Black Masses in the press, came out in 1904, written by the pornographer Alphonse Gallais, *Les Mémoires du Baron Jacques*, in which Baron Jacque's mother takes his virginity at an early age [Byron lost his to a maid at age 9]. Baron Jacques goes on to deflower his own young boys, copulating with them on his mother's skeleton!

For Fersen's times what he did was highly

titillating, and because minors were involved he was sentenced to five months in prison. As he was no longer welcome by family and friends, he exchanged Paris's cloudy skies for sunny Capri. But before we get to his exploits there, perhaps a word on his *oeuvre*.

In 1902 he published a collection of poems called *L'Hymnaire d'Adonis*, in which we find the poem *Treize Ans*: At age 13, blond with precocious eyes full of desire and emotion, his lips already streetwise, he's in the study hall where all the boys are reading, bent over their books, while only he, in a corner, is going through randy poems by Musset. As the supervisor goes by he hides what he's doing and pretends to be hard at work, but when the coast's clear he brings out his book and, turning into the shadows so as not to be seen, he slips his hand into his pocket where a hole leads to his toy that, lost in licentious thoughts, he fondles for a long, long time. [*Treize ans, blondin aux yeux précoces, Qui disent le désir et l'émoi, Lèvres, ayant je ne sais quoi De mutin, de vicieux, de gosse. Il lit; dans la salle ils sont Tous penchés à écrire un thème, Lui seul dans un coin lit quand même, Des vers de Musset, polissons; Le pion passe, vite il se cache, Semblant travailler avec feu, À quelque devoir nébuleux, Très propre, soigné et sans tache, Puis calmé, le moment d'après, Reprend tout rose sa lecture, Se met à changer de posture, Pour être de l'ombre plus près; Coule ses mains, sans qu'on devine, Dans sa poche percée d'un trou, Et là longuement fait joujou, Rêveur de voluptés félines!*]

Sex was a daily and nightly pastime in boarding schools. Besides his school experiences, Fersen is known to have loved a young British boy from Eton during a summer holiday on the island of Jersey.

In 1904 he wrote a novel entitled *Lord Lillian*, which is about his trial and is dedicated to the judge that collected the information [in France a single judge collects facts for-and-against a person accused of a crime, and is supposed to present the facts, neutrally, to the court. This neutrality rarely takes place and is the cause of hundreds of years of injustice, but the power of the judiciary is such that a new system cannot be adopted].

The main character in Fersen's book is Renold, Lord Lyllian [named after his brother], who lost his adulterous mother and beloved father before the age of 17. He falls into the hands of a certain Skilde [Oscar Wilde], the author of *The Portrait of Miriam Green* [*Dorian Gray*]. Skilde farms the boy out to take care of the sexual needs of Skilde's clients but following the suicide of a member of one of Skilde's orgies he flees, while Skilde is imprisoned and condemned to hard labor.

Renold tours the world, going from lover to lover until he meets a Swedish poet Axel Ansen [Axel from his father's name] who unfortunately dies young. Renold goes to Paris where he creates Black Masses with naked choirboys, one of which dies. Fersen has Renold proclaim that the Masses were simply to excite the boys so that they would find shared love among themselves [which is certainly what happened in the case of Fersen in his real life in Paris]. Fersen is thought to have put himself into four of his characters, all of whom make love together at some point in the novel, and of course his greatest sexual partner was the poet Axel.

Renold finally decides to give up boy-love and marries a girl. In real life Fersen had been on the verge of marrying a very rich young lady who, despite his begging to see her, refused him following his trial.

His book *Youth* was dedicated to his very young lover Nino Cesarini, ''More beautiful than the light of Rome.''

It concerns the painter Robert, age 23, who is in love with Nino, a 16-year-old seminary student. But a priest is also in love with Nino *and* a girl, a girl Nino is in love with. Finally, the girl dies and Nino himself becomes a priest.

He wrote a poem entitled *So Sang Marsyas* which related the true story of his belovèd Nino who, in Venice, met and appreciated a girl, Alexandrine, who liked him so much she followed him to Capri where he bedded her. In the poem Fersen asked, ''How many tears must I shed to wash away her kisses?''

In 1909 he published 12 editions of a cultural magazine called *Akademos*, a total of 2,000 pages, that was said to have been about 10% homosexual. It failed after a year.

Le baiser de Narcisse, The Kiss of Narcissus: Again, due to the times, one was cautious in what one wrote, especially if one wished a wide audience. In this book the most daring sentence evokes the hero coming upon a group of youths, whose tunics of transparent linen revealed their young and muscular forms. ''Extremely young, he undid his tunic that he let fall to the ground, and in a pose equal to that of a god, he remained still, while the sun spread its golden rays over the mother-of-pearl forms of his flesh. His muscular legs rose like two columns of alabaster to his flat stomach and his precocious virility. He then sang and danced, in his glorious nudity.''

The boy in question was Milès, born in Bithynia, the birthplace of Antinous. As a child he was already so beautiful that people turned to watch him pass, ''for in those times the people knew how to appreciate beauty and a boy's splendid forms, a time before Antinous, born to please an emperor, and they all exclaimed, This boy is for Zeus, for they knew of the gods' love for earthlings.''

The boy is taken as a slave to Athens by the architect Scopas who falls in love with him and frees him but is not given the boy's love in return, and so he dies of despair. The lad, by then 15, poses for the painter Ictinos for a fresco of Ganymede, Zeus's love mate. Milès then travels until he comes to a pond into which he finally sees a boy as beautiful as he. He leans over to kiss the image, his fingers slip … and the book ends.

Now back to Fersen's life.

Rich but rejected, he withdrew to Capri, noted for being a homosexual refuge since Tiberius withdrew there 2000 years previously. Fersen built a palace, the Villa Lysis, facing Tiberius's Villa Jovis, a neoclassical affair of Ionic columns, an entrance with an atrium, and bedrooms with wondrous views of the palace gardens, the distant sea and Mount Vesuvius. There he surrounded himself with island boys until he was requested to leave when he brought in boys from elsewhere, in competition with the homegrown crop, a loss of income for the lads and their families. The Caprian boys in question have been immortalized by a succession of photographers and painters, their bodies caressed by generations of financially fortunate lovers of boys.

A basement apartment, called the Chinese Room, was dedicated to opium smoking, where Fersen contented himself with up to 40 pipes a day, a huge but supposedly not unheard of quantity for addicts. Opium depresses the urge to have sex, although it can be used to postpone an orgasm, allowing more enjoyment before eventual ejaculation. Taking 40 pipes meant he was having no orgasms at all. It was in the Chinese Room that, in 1923, at age 43, his health failing, he drank a mortal cocktail of cocaine and champagne, certainly entering eternity with an ecstatic Wow!

[The entire history of French homosexuality, and far more risqué drawings by Cocteau, can be found in my book *French Homosexuality*.]

PART FIVE

THE ROARING TWENTIES MADE IN AMERICA

Hollywood

The epicenter of American homosexuality during the roaring Twenties was clearly Hollywood, long before San Francisco's Castro district and Brad Davis's selling himself in the streets of N.Y., prior to his stardom thanks to *Midnight Express* (5) or Warhol's' Factory and its wall-to-wall sucking and fucking (33).

Hollywood was a wasteland that the extraordinary H.J. Whitley came upon in 1886. Something about the land and terrain inspired him to found a town, the name derived when he saw a Chinaman seated on a horse-drawn wagon loaded with wood. When Whitley asked him what he was doing, the man answered ''I holly-wood'', hauling wood. The land on which the encounter took place was owned by a rancher, E.C. Hurd, from whom Whitley bought 480 acres. With investors, he formed the Los Angeles Pacific Boulevard and Development Company. Located 10 miles from downtown Los Angeles, the land Whitley purchased consisted of shrubs, some vineyards, citrus groves, barley and bean fields, little to attract investment and home owners, scarce reason for Los Angeles's 102,000 residents to move to a forsaken dustbowl reachable only by horse.

Whitely decided that he could attract investor by constructing a luxurious hotel, an oasis of three acres of gardens, palms, sycamores, oaks, eucalyptus, California pepper trees and endless lawns that he named Hollywood Hotel.

Tycoon Burton Green had purchased land at the foot of the Santa Monica Mountains, where he built a mansion, and felt that the best way to attract buyers for his lots would be the construction of a hotel, most likely adopting the idea from H.J. Whitley and the success of the Hollywood Hotel. He named it Beverly Hills Hotel and chose as his motto ''our guests are entitled to the best of everything regardless of cost" (1). Green publicized the perfect climate found in California, the 290 days of sun per year, and lack of humidity and snow. The *Los Angeles Times* sent free newspapers to the East Coast, in midwinter, reporting on the Tournament of Roses parade in balmy downtown Los Angeles. The decision to go West was aided by competition between two rival train lines, the Santa Fe Railroad and the Southern Pacific, prices at times as low as $1.

    The burgeoning film industry and its stars as numerous as those in the heavens [claimed film moguls] did the rest. The population of Los Angeles continued to explode. The hotel opened in 1912 and attracted actors, largely thanks to its 23 bungalows where they could fuck in discretion, a sexual bonanza fueled by the first trains [later trains and buses] pulling in with optimistic youths certain to be tomorrow's stars, mostly girls who had won hometown beauty contests and now wanted to cash in on their looks, each acquainted with the biography of this or that movie star who had been unknown until discovered working in this or that drugstore or hash house. There were so many girls that they were had for just the promise of what a guy connected with the studios [or pretending to be so] could do for them, while the boys, fewer in number, had to really be taken on, at the very least as extras, for them to open their fly.

    Actresses wanted their husbands for themselves, while millions of years of evolution [its purpose the survival of the species (9)] pushed men to sow their seed to the four winds, fidelity a masculine impossibility. The discreet encounters in the bungalows saved scores of marriages, and generated so much money that the Garden of Allah would soon be open, offering villas with even greater discretion, patrolled by guards to make certain that Allah clients were not disturbed.

The Beverly Hills Hotel.
In the 1920s one had to reserve a table weeks in advance at the Beverly Hills Hotel and white-clad cabana boys were paid to page poolside patrons, ''Calling Mister Romano!'', as well as wipe up semen from the floor of the changing rooms, half of which was often their own, a way of earning dollars that had great buying power back then. The pull of flagrant easily-available sex brought men out on horseback under the blazing sun, their lust fueled by sugary alcoholic drinks and the juicy, spicy hamburgers for which the hotel was famous.

The luxury of the Beverly Hills Hotel drew the likes of Douglas Fairbanks and his wife Mary Pickford, the king and queen of cinema, who built what some called a lodge, others a mansion, Pickfair, on land above the hotel. When the construction began in 1920 the land was worth $500 a lot, by the time it was completed, five years later, lots in the vicinity sold for $30,000. Alas for Mary, Fairbanks's sexual escapades were discovered, leading to their divorce. Their son, the superhumanly handsome Douglas Fairbanks Jr., was a chip off the old block except for his omnisexual orientation (3). When his wife Joan Crawford was questioned about his whereabouts by one of her guests, William Haines, the ever-candid Crawford replied, "He's out butt-fucking Larry Olivier." This left Crawford free to console herself with Clark Gable, a man who had himself been butt-fucked by the reigning star of the times, William Haines, in order to get his first role in a film, which in a way was lucky for Gable whose ears were big, his breath bad, and reportedly, his dick so small that it attracted few takers.

Haines

At age 36 William Haines was arrested for assaulting a 6-year-old child that he had picked up on the beach, had taken home, showered with, and then, on his bed, took the whole of the child's apparatus in his mouth. As a famous president claimed that he committed a sexual act because he could, because he was powerful enough to get away with it, such was the case of the man few of us have ever heard of, a man so well known, so famous, that he was probably the only man on earth who fucked Clark Gable, with Gable's consent when Gable found out it was the only way to get a role in a film.

Haines was a rarity, too, in daring to flout his difference, and this in the face of L.B. Mayer, head of MGM, a homophobe [or more probably a man who just couldn't understand why a guy wouldn't want a woman--of whom Mayer had many]. One of Haines's fellow workers stated, ''He may have worked hard eight to ten hours a day, but he pursued young men--especially sailors--for at least eight hours most nights.'' (11)

When finally forced out of movies, Haines turned to decorating the homes of the rich, at which he was said to have been excellent.

So today Haines is known for Gable, as during the Renaissance the artist Torrigiano--even though he was the first to introduce Renaissance art into England--is known to *cognoscenti* mainly as the man who broke Michelangelo's nose in a lover's spat (8).

Haines reigned during the days of silent films, so a list of his film successes will mean nothing today, as even Gloria Swanson's are forgotten. Haines ran away from home in Virginia at age 14, already 6' tall, and already with a boyfriend. Both went to Richmond where they found work at a Du Pont plant. Haines made it to N.Y. at age 16 and worked in a rubber factory. He then sold himself (6), and his friends at the time said he couldn't get enough sex. He returned to Virginia for two years before heading back to the Big Apple.

He took pride in being a rent boy for what society had best in men and women, and was known for being "rascally handsome and devilishly funny," says William J. Mann is his excellent book on Haines, *Wisecracker*.

He got to Hollywood as did many good-looking boys then and today, met and mated Valentino, as did everyone else of beauty. He had actor Ramón Novarro and producer George Cukor, yet his best friends were women, Alla Nazimova and Joan Crawford, Crawford who told him that her husband, Douglas Fairbanks Jr., was in an adjoining room fucking Laurence Olivier. Very early on he did something unknown among homosexuals, he found a boy, Jimmy Shields, who brought him contentment, he said, and with whom he would spend the rest of his life [and with whom he would share his hustlers (5)]. He became intimate with Gary Cooper who had had sex with Laurence Olivier too, and told Haines that he couldn't understand the Englishman who was flaming with desire one moment, a cold fish the next. The only person Haines couldn't stand was Garbo, because although Haines claimed to be a free soul, he nonetheless got married in order to still rumors concerning his homosexuality, whereas Garbo did exactly what she wished, with whomever she wished.

Haines nearly did so too, especially sexually, but when Mayer had to bail him out of jail for turning up drunk with still another sailor or soldier, he told Haines to stop his messing around or he'd tear up his contract. Haines chose the freedom to fuck whomever he wanted.

Then in 1936 came his arrest and trial for child molestation. Amazingly, the author of *Wisecracker* found the boy involved, 60 years later. Yes, the man said, he blew me, but as I told them back then, it didn't do me any harm.

Haines had been found *not* guilty due to incredible circumstances: In court the 6-year-old boy was asked if the man who had touched him was in the room?

Sixty years later the gentleman explained: Haines was sitting across from me. I wanted to tell them all that the man was at the table. So when the prosecutor asked if he was in the court, I said "No", wanting to add, he's *at that table*. But the defense immediately rose and asked to have the case dismissed.

And it was.

Nothing is left of Haines's films. Nothing of his humor. Like Torrigiano who broke Michelangelo's nose, he's known only for anally abusing a man who needed a role in a film, and cruising a child whose parents had left him unattended on a beach.

The dining room of the Beverly Hills Hotel served 500, and among the hotel's tropical foliage were fountains, a stable with 25 Kentucky horses and tennis courts, over which presided the king of tennis, William Tilden, three-time Wimbledon winner, the World No. 1 player from 1920 through 1925. He was invited to the homes of Chaplin and Fairbanks, Jr. and others, where he offered lessons. Tilden traveled by train from the East Coast to the Pacific Coast in the company of underage tennis ball boys, which would eventually lead to his imprisonment. [Tilden's life is fully covered in my book *BOYS*.]

In 1910 D.W. Griffith made *In Old California*, 17-minutes in length, the first Hollywood film. The first studio, the Nestor Company, opened behind a tavern, followed by Paramount, Warner, RKO and Columbia. By 1930 Hollywood was producing 300 films a year, and already, in 1923, the fancy Hollywood sign was set up, its purpose to advertise a housing development called Hollywoodland. The electrified sign was Whitley's brainchild, suggested to the developer of Hollywoodland because Whitley had used one to advertise his own development, Whitley Heights, with great success. The Hollywoodland sign cost a whopping $21,000 [$320,000 today, 2019] and was studded with 4,000 lightbulbs. The sign flashed ''HOLLY'' and ''WOOD'' and ''LAND'' lit up individually, and then the whole (1). [Supplicant actors didn't have long to succeed before their looks faded and the sun turned their skin to leather. Many turned to prostitution, drugs and one, Lillian Entwistle, jumped to her death from the top of the Hollywood sign ''H''.]

Griffith Park

Architect Wilbur Cook was responsible for the layout of several towns and parks, one of which was Griffith Park, donated to the city of Los Angeles in 1896 by Griffith J. Griffith, a property developer who served two years in prison for shooting his wife in the face [she survived]. Far larger and more rugged and untamed than N.Y.'s Central Park, Griffith Park became the main cruising area of California, where during both World Wars soldiers and sailors flocked for the mutual comfort of a shared ejaculation. It also served as the backdrop to D.W. Griffith's battle scenes in his epic *Birth of a Nation*.

The Greystone Mansion

The Greystone Mansion was another noted Hollywood landmark, built by oil tycoon Edward Doheny for his son Ned in 1929, four months before Ned's death, leaving a wife and five children.

On the 16th of February 1929, Ned was found in the bedroom of his secretary, Hugh Plunkett, Ned's gun wiped clean of prints between the bodies. Ned was denied a Catholic burial, as is the case for suicides, yet the official report stated that Plunkett had shot him before killing himself, either due to a mental disorder or because Ned had refused to give him a raise. Both were buried at Forest Lawn Memorial Park, in close proximity.

The reader may be familiar with the life of Edward Doheny, Ned's father, the biography of whom was the basis of the ultra-violent movie *There Will Be Blood*, the last, grisly scene of which was filmed in Ned's Greystone Mansion, in the downstairs two-lane bowling alley Doheny-*père* had built for him.

Many believe that the motive for the deaths was the Teapot Dome Scandal [as huge then as Watergate today], when Doheny-*père* sent Ned, accompanied by Plunkett, with a $100,000 cash bribe for United States Secretary of the Interior Albert Fall, in exchange for Fall leasing oil land on a naval reserve in Wyoming at extremely low cost [in all, Doheny paid Fall $385,000, $5,500,000 today, 2019]. During the trial that followed, Doheny-*père* and Ned feared that Plunkett would tell the truth under interrogation, and tried to shut him up by having him voluntarily enter an insane asylum. Plunkett was certain that, once inside, Doheny-*père* would use his wealth to have him put away for life. Ned thusly killed him to protect his father, and then committed suicide, a scenario that worked: due to public sympathy over his losing his son, Doheny-*père* was found innocent of bribery, while Albert Fall was found guilty of accepting Doheny's money (!), and went to jail for a year.

Ned's wife had heard a shot and, bizarrely, phoned the family doctor, not the police. Both maintained that Plunkett opened the door to his room for them, holding a handgun, but then shut it. Moments later they heard a shot, both bodies found on the floor in pools of blood. Three hours later the police were summoned. Ned's wife admitted having moved the bodies when forensics proved that Plunkett had initially been facedown outside the bedroom door, cigarette in hand, a bullet in his back, the shot having been fired from a distance. Further forensic evidence attested that Ned, age 35, had been inside the room, an empty whisky glass nearby, gunpowder marks on his forehead. He and Plunkett had been inseparable friends from boyhood, Plunkett, Ned's lover, taken on as valet, driver and finally secretary.

Hearst

William Randolph Hearst built his sumptuous San

Simeon Castle, about which Bernard Shaw said it best: ''The castle was what God would have built if he had had the money.'' The castle pool was the greatest and most beautiful to have ever existed, and the guest houses that surrounded the castle were in themselves palaces, replete with every luxury except for kitchens, as Hearst didn't believe in loafing around; if his guests wanted food, they could make their way to San Simeon. Each mansion guest had its servants, the first question asked to each, when the guests woke up the first morning there was, ''Could we have some coffee, please'', ''we'' because the guests were seldom unaccompanied. ''You'll have to go to the castle'' was the response, the servant prepared to be injuriously rebuked [which Hearst wouldn't stand for: always impeccably polite, he supported those who worked for him as tenaciously as if they were family--better than if they were family, because as a father to his five sons he seems to have been a pitiful failure]. Said his mistress Marion Davies, ''W.R. [Hearst] does not approve of breakfast in bed.''

While one would think that Hearst, due to his wealth, was basically conservative, in point of fact he was a liberal democrat. He was also prudish and discouraged sexual relations, obliging a lot of stealthy movement between castle rooms and around the grounds after Hearst had retired to bed. He had his mistresses, of whom Marion Davies was the reigning queen, and let people do what they basically wanted to do, although not under his roof. He put Cary Grant and Randolph Scott in adjoining suits, surely without contemplating, a single nanosecond, what was physically going on between them (27). On the other hand, he encouraged friendships between Marion and Robert Vignola and Bill Haines because he knew that both were exclusively homosexual, so unlike the British and the Italians who were most often omnisexual. Vignola, like Valentino, was born in a poor Italian village, but unlike Valentino who came to America under his own power, Vignola emigrated at age 3 with his parents. Trained as a barber at age 14, he got odd jobs in theaters, his stage debut in 1901. He acted in a number of silent films before becoming a director, churning out 110 pictures from 1911 to 1937. He made Marion Davies a star by choosing her for *When Knighthood Was in Flower*. He gave Valentino a cameo role in *Seventeen*. Haines has his own chapter.

Hearst developed "giant newspaper headlines over lurid stories lecturing crime, corruption, sex, and innuendo" (1), although he was outdone by James Gordon Bennett of the New York *Herald* who paid Henry Stanley to find Livingston. Bennett too believed in headlines, like the one reserved for the New York visit of the nattily dressed Haitian ambassador: "A GORGEOUS NIGGER" (26).

Another man to make the headlines was John Brinkley, the Roaring Twenties' major quack, who increased men's virility by inserting a goat testicle or two into the scrotum of men willing to shell out $750 per gonad. *Los Angeles Times* owner Harry Chandler was purportedly among them (27); the front page of the April 9, 1922 edition of the *Los Angeles Times* read:
NEW LIFE IN GLANDS – MEN VICTIMS OF INCURABLE DISEASES ARE CURED
During this time, in Chicago, Harold McCormick,

multi-millionaire heir to the International Harvester fortune, received, reported the *New York Time* of June 18, 1922, the testicle of ''a virile youth of formidable stature and highly developed physique, carefully selected for his physical attainments. It is hinted around the hospital that the unidentified youth has acquired some of McCormick's wealth in return for his sacrifice.''

The Scandal that Shocked the Roaring Twenties

The Leopold/Loeb scandal took place in 1924 with the murder of 14-year-old Bobby Franks by 19-year-old Nathan Leopold and 18-year-old Richard Loeb, Bobby's cousin. The murderers were defended by Clarence Darrow, a god among lawyers, who took the case because he was a staunch opponent to the death penalty. The definitive history of the affair is found in Simon Battz's must-read, *For the Thrill of It*, 2008, the title the reason why Leopold and Loeb took the boy's precious life. Leopold is most cited by writers as the driving force of the cowardly assassination, a boy said to have known 15 languages, including Sanskrit, a Phi Beta Kappa who had graduated from the University of Chicago at age 18, his IQ 210 [although there are, apparently, discrepancies between the tests of IQs then and now]. Richard Loeb was 6 months younger and had skipped a number of grades, which allowed him to graduate from the University of Michigan at age 17. He was outgoing, sociable, athletic, serious in his mating with girls. Both boys were homosexually intimate, Loeb claiming that he had let Leopold have his way because he was so insistent, maintaining that ''I could get along without it. The actual sex act is rather unimportant to me," a quote from Baatz, although Loeb's later enthusiasm for sex in prison belies this.

Both boys came from homes of wealth, freeing them from financial restraints, and their intellectual prowess spared them the grind of study. Both sought other means of excitation, especially Loeb, while Leopold was obsessed with Nietzsche and his superman that, in ways, he'd found in Loeb. He was perfectly willing to be Loeb's slave, and when Loeb decided to add spice to their lives by acts of vandalism, arson and theft [especially the fraternities of Loeb's friends], Leopold readily agreed. When Loeb suggested committing the perfect crime, it was Leopold who justified it by stating, "On account of certain superior qualities inherent in [us, we were] exempt from the ordinary laws that govern men."

The murder took seven months of preparation, proof in itself of the serious approach to the act, the boys even coming up with the idea of hiring a car under a false name. Spotting Bobby Franks as he left the Harvard School for Boys, Loeb persuaded him to enter the car where he wanted Franks to examine a new tennis racket he'd bought, something Bobby willingly did because he'd often played tennis with Loeb at the Loeb residence. The boy sat in front, while Loeb, seated behind, struck him with a chisel, a chisel bought for the purpose. They took the body to a field 25 miles away, stripped it naked, doused the genitals and face with hydrochloric acid to prevent identification, and wedged it into a culvert. Why they had chosen a chisel, and why they destroyed Bobby's boyhood, are unknown. Incredibly, a pair of Leopold's glasses fell from his jacket pocket, the expense and uniqueness of which led to their capture, glasses that Leopold explained he'd dropped the preceding week while out birdwatching. As for an alibi, both said they'd picked up girls from the street in Leopold's car, whom they'd dropped off after being serviced. The Leopold family chauffer later swore that the car had not left the garage during the time of the killing.

Richard Loeb, Bobby Franks and Nathan Leopold.

Loeb confessed first, followed by Leopold, each blaming the other for giving the fatal blows.

The newspapers stated that Darrow had accepted the case for a million dollars, that Darrow claimed was a dishonorable slur, as he'd received only $70,000 [worth $1,048,538 in 2019]. His closing argument lasted 24 hours, in which he only asked that the boy's lives be spared. Both received life terms, plus 99 years. A month later Richard Loeb's father was downed by a heart attack.

In prison the wealthy Loeb could buy whatever he wanted, have lunch and dinner in his cell, and wear civilian clothes. Guards gave him keys to certain rooms where he could take the men he paid for sex. He lusted for a new boy, age 21, whom he told to meet him in the showers. The boy in question, James Day, was highly unstable, victim of a disastrous childhood, who, before going to the showers, borrowed a razor knife that he used to stab Richard Loeb 46 times, Loeb's blood and life drained way with the shower water. Because anyone who testified against Day in court would have had his throat slit on return to prison, Day was acquitted, claiming that it was Loeb who had attacked him with the knife when Day refused his advances, a knife he'd wrestled from Loeb's hands.

As for Nathan Leopold, he wrote a book, *Life Plus 99 Years,* while in prison, where he was a model inmate, teacher and hospital volunteer, adding 12 languages to the 15 languages some sources claim he already possessed. He was released in 1958 and set up the Leopold Foundation to aid emotionally disturbed, retarded or delinquent youths. He exiled himself to Puerto Rico where he worked as a laboratory assistant, dedicating his time to doing research on leprosy [in prison he had inoculated himself with malaria pathogens in order to help researchers find a treatment].

He died of a heart attack at age 66, his last donation his corneas.

The Kiss

One of the notable films of the Roaring Twenties was the 1927 *Wings*, the first-ever to be given an Academy Award for Best Picture, and the first to show a kiss between men, and not just any men. Richard Arlen and Buddy Rogers were the finest Hollywood had to offer in male beauty.

Richard Arlen, 1899-1976, was a pilot during W.W. I. A laborer on oil fields in Texas and Oklahoma, he decided to try his luck as an actor in Los Angeles, but so numerous were good-looking aspirants that he wound up working as a delivery boy, which led to his having a motorcycle accident while delivering films to Paramount. One of the people who rushed to help him was a producer who, not insensitive to his face and athletic body, nor to the pain caused by his broken leg, got him work as an extra when he was back on his feet. He made the transition from silent films to talkies, his greatest performance coming in *Wings* where he played opposite Buddy Rogers, a role for which Arlen, as a pilot, was imminently prepared.

Buddy and Arlen

Charles ''Buddy'' Rogers, 1904-1999, was, like Arlen, a pilot, and both were university students [rare at the time]. Buddy's background was musical. He played several instruments and made records for Columbia and Victor in which he sang, and was physically so cute that he was dubbed "America's Boy Friend." Also like Arlen, he became a flight training instructor during W.W. II. His talent and looks brought him to the attention of Mary Pickford who divorced Douglas Fairbanks to marry him, a marriage that lasted 42 years, until her death. Buddy followed at age 94, while Arlen made it to 77.

In the film *Wings* both Arlen and Rogers were in love with the same woman, played by Clara Bow, but as writer Kevin Sessums put it, "neither showed as much love for her as they did for each other."

The Kiss.
The scene can be seen on YouTube, the most affectionate kiss in cinema and in life that I've ever witnessed, unfeigned tenderness that brought tears to my eyes.

The Garden of Allah

It was the best of times, when the planets aligned to place in one garden, that of Allah, the most beautiful representatives of humanity the world had ever seen, united in one location, during Hollywood's Roaring Twenties homosexual heyday: Laurence Olivier, Errol Flynn, David Niven, Tyrone Power, Valentino, Ramón Novarro, to name a very few, whose bungalows had their own entrances, and a pool, the largest existent in Hollywood, for skinny dipping and sheltered corners where untanned buttocks, a white parenthesis in deeply bronzed bodies, were lighted by the first-ever underwater illumination, a pleasure for those in the wee hours who caught the humping, and, perhaps, even the highlighted milky clouds released by the last-minute withdrawals that assured the actors they would not face suits for child support.

There were orgies, hustlers (5) and prostitutes, especially during the war years when one lived fast and furious because one didn't know how long one would remain alive, hot and fast because the studios were dishing out the money, and around the Crash of '29 boys and girls could be bought for the proverbial Hershey Bar.

The Garden of Allah was located on Sunset Boulevard, which ran from Downtown Los Angeles to the Pacific Ocean, an ancient cattle trail 22 miles long. Sections were still dirt roads at the time of our story, with actors riding to Alla's mansion horseback from Paramount studios, and the area was calm, although night life had begun to settle in: prostitution, a strip joint named Pandora's Box, liquor stores to supply the denizens of the Garden, a pharmacy, Schwab's, to care for their hangovers and sexually transmitted diseases.

The part of Sunset Boulevard where the Garden of

Allah was located was known as the Strip, a mile-and-a-half long, which, at the time, was not an incorporated part of the City of Los Angeles, meaning it was not under the heavy hand and scrutiny of the Los Angeles Police Department. Gambling was unlawful within the city limits but thrived outside, as did speakeasies during Prohibition. Actors danced at Ciro's, the Mocambo and the Trocadero, benevolently smiled upon by gagsters Bugsy Siegel and Mickey Cohen who owned or had shares in many of the most famous clubs and restaurants. Wealthy, with all the girls they wanted at their beck and call, there was little reason either gangster would have stepped foot in the Garden, nor would their extremely influential and well-known sidekick, George Raft, although, on the other hand, all three were known for occasional slumming, and Siegel was star struck. Bugsy's mistress Virginia Hill was not only a regular guest, she was said to have blackmailed the men she seduced at the Garden. Readers who are familiar with the life of Siegel know that he was assassinated by his mafia friends when the casino he was building, the Flamingo, went millions over budget. Virginia had stashed away a purported $3 million that she had creamed from the top and placed in Switzerland. The mafia gave her the choice of either returning it or receiving a bullet through the eye, as had Siegel. She returned it all, before later committing suicide.

A mansion had been built on the site by real-estate developer William H. Hay in 1913, at 8152 Sunset Boulevard to be exact, and consisted of 12 rooms, which was turned over to actress Alla Nazimova five years later. Alla, as she was universally called, was born in Yalta under Dickensian conditions: divorced parents, shabby boarding schools and foster homes. She studied acting in Moscow where she became a successful actress, there and in Saint Petersburg. During a tour of America she decided to stay in New York where, incredibly, she learned English well enough to not only act in Broadway productions but to become extremely popular, so much so that a theater was named for her. Offered a contract by Metro Pictures [soon to be MGM] she began at $13,000 a week in 1917 [$245,000 today]. Soon wealthy, she became an American citizen in 1927. In a later film she played Tyrone Power's mother in his 1941 *Blood and Sand*.

She is credited with having invented the phrase ''sewing circle'', code for her gatherings of lesbian actresses in her digs at the Garden of Allah, among whom were Barbara Stanwyck, Joan Crawford, Garbo and Tallulah Bankhead, as well as the writer Dorothy Parker. Although she had numerous heterosexual love affairs, Alla launched the careers of two of Rudolph Valentino's wives, lesbians Valentino married for public consumption [not private].

Nazimova leased the Hay mansion in 1918 and bought it outright the following year, it and two-and-a-half acres of lush fruit trees and tropical plants. Facing bankruptcy in 1926, and looking for a steady income for her retirement, she borrowed $1.5 million and had 25 villas built, Spanish style, and a huge pool in the shape of the Black Sea, in memory of her Crimean birthplace, although some sources claim that the shape was suggested to her by her astrologer, conform in some recondite way to her horoscope. The grand opening took place in 1927, with a packed attendance in part thanks to a brochure she had sent out to the studios promising an ''atmosphere of exclusive refinement'' to those who rented her villas, one of which, Villa 24, she lived in till her death at age 66, in 1945, from coronary thrombosis. The Garden closed in 1959 and the furnishings sold at a public auction, each buyer assured that the bed he bought had belonged to Errol Flynn.

Rudolph Valentino

A regular at the Hollywood and Beverly Hills hotels, one of Alla's first most notable visitors was Valentino, from around 1924 to his death in 1926. He rode over horseback from the Paramount studio lot, and during one luncheon he met Alla's set designer, Winifred Shaughnessy, who was also Alla's lover. When Valentino decided he needed a wife for publicity reasons he chose Shaughnessy, which greatly angered Alla but opened up a whole new life of wealth for Winifred who changed her name to Natcha Rambova, and it was as such that she tried out for roles in films, landing a part in *When Love Grows Cold*. She eventually calmed Alla by frequently attending her lesbian sewing circles. Alla had also previously introduced Valentino to his first wife, who returned to live on the Garden grounds with Alla after her divorce from Valentino. Rambova wrote that she would treasure her honeymoon with Valentino all her life [Valentino had often said he was an ace at handling his 10 inches, and could bring pleasure to whomever he ''honored'']. She wanted to continue her career, her major disagreement with Valentino who wanted a son and wanted her home to care for Valentino himself. His Italian male chauvinism eventually abandoned him to the extent that it was she who ruled the roost, deciding even the roles in films he would accept to play. Her influence was so disruptive that only when she was banned from the studios did Valentino find work again. After Valentino's death she remarried, founded a dress shop on Fifth Avenue, N.Y., taught Spiritualism and Egyptology, passing away at age 66 from heart failure, remembered from then on as Valentino's second wife, Mrs. Valentino.

Rodolfo Alfonso Raffaello Pierre Filibert Guglielmi di Valentina d'Antonguolla, ''Valentino'', was born in 1895. He didn't start off with a life as incredibly adventurous as Errol Flynn's or David Niven's, but he was rough and undisciplined, sent from school to school for being uncontrollable. At first he chose agriculture as his life's work and went to school in Genoa where at 5' 11'' he took up weight-lifting and football. His father had left him money he used to travel to Paris where he went to clubs like the Alcazar and picked up the Apache, a wild dance in which the barely dressed girl was hoisted about, flung like a ragdoll, slapping the male while he threatened her with a knife, she a prostitute, he her pimp. Getting a hard-on with a man showing him the movements, the man loaned Valentino his wife to straighten the boy out, but in the end Valentino got the man.

As he had in Marseille, he found work at Maxim's as a dancer, paid by women per dance and beyond the dance floor servicing. As they were rich, and as he later stated that fucking had always come easily to him, he made good money. He specialized in the tango and had his trousers tailored to show off his muscular buttocks and extensive manhood. Soon named the Italian Stallion, he thrilled the ladies, who requested private dance lessons. His reputation was augmented when it became known that he was too much of a mouthful for most of them, but just right for a pussy needing stretching.

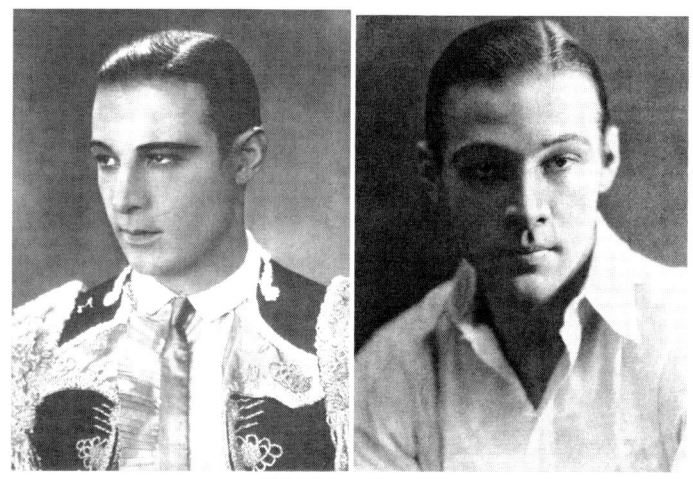

Valentino

One of Valentino's rich clients was a woman who shot her husband dead, and Rudy, afraid of being dragged into the trial, fled to California. In Los Angeles he hooked up with an actor who convinced him to try out for work as a studio extra.

He became a member of the Torch Club, at around $1,000 a month, that had a special room, # 23, above which was a two-way mirror. New boys were given the room where they fucked in full view of a hidden audience, jacking off. The first boy he went into the room with was Richard Barthelmess, both unaware of the voyeurs. Richard later posed nude for friends and was said to have been huge. Rudy met producers at the club and got numerous small roles. He was soon servicing actresses for money, several a day, and still had enough for Richard whom he continued to see.

Valentino got the chief role in *The Four Horsemen of the Apocalypse* during which Novarro, a bit-player, told him that Valentino was the love of his life. In thanks Valentino gave Novarro a 10'' bronze sculpture of his cock, the one Novarro purportedly choked to death on at the end of his kidnapping/murder, whose story follows. During a party Valentino and his girlfriend were introduced as Snow White and Mr. 7 Inches, so the exact size of his manhood is unknown.

The success of *The Four Horsemen of the Apocalypse* rocketed him to fame, but he was so imbued with himself that he made increasing demands for more money, causing bad blood among directors and costing him good roles, some of which went to Novarro. He left Metro for Famous Players where his contract went from $350 a week to $750, this during the depression when one earned a dollar a day, if lucky.

His film *The Sheik* was taken from an English book found nearly pornographic, about a woman kidnapped by an Arab who used her for his sexual pleasure in his tent, telling her that she had it better with him than his men, and then the shocking discloser that she ended up liking ''it''. The amusing aspect is that the female lead gave interviews comparing Latin lovers to Americans, although in reality she preferred women and was thought to have been a virgin [to men at least].

His fan mail exploded, with women requesting pubic hair clippings and men underwear he ejaculated in--in return for money. He married. Divorced. And immediately married again, so rapidly that the first marriage hadn't come through and he was indicted for bigamy. He got out of it when his new wife declared their marriage had not been consummated, and was thusly null and void.

His next film was the one he preferred, *Blood and Sand*, he as a matador. He was 26 and apparently loved to wear the matador costume from then on as a preliminary to sex.

In the film *Young Rajah* Valentino played a student who, in one scene where the rowers were wearing shorts and carrying a boat over their heads, was bawled out by the director who thought he was sporting a boner as a prank, and ordered him to take a cold shower. Valentino lowered the shorts to prove that he was in his normal flaccid state.

Valentino was said to have had such magnetism that even homophobes wanted to have sex with him, wrote Jacques Hébertot, whose pleasure was touring French streets to pick up boys that he turned into actors. Hébertot's greatest discovery was Gérard Philipe, one of France's truly great and beloved artists. Hébertot introduced Valentino to André Daven that Hébertot said was the world's most beautiful boy. Stuck on himself, Daven told the great Valentino that if he wanted him he'd have to give him a role in one of his films. Valentino replied that he'd give the boy a role in *all* his films, an anecdote revealed by David Bret in his *Valentino*, a wonderful biography.

Valentino in the middle, Daven on the right [sorry, it's the best photo I can find].

In 1923, at age 28, Valentino signed a contract with United Artists that paid $10,000 a week and 42% of United Artists' profits, plus a bungalow, a maid, a dresser and a chef. The only provision was that his wife, the harridan Rambova, have no say whatsoever concerning the films and the filming of the films. He signed, especially as Daven was still at his side. [After Valentino's death Daven returned to Paris and to Hébertot, and then literally disappeared from the face of the planet.]

Valentino bought a boat, packed with boys, usually nude, and went to Catalina Island. The fun and games continued at his home, Falcon Lair, where Valentino especially liked to fuck on the roof of his car. Valentino declared a "no fuck Friday", Bret tells us, reserved for outings to things like boxing matches. But as soon as midnight struck, it was back home and orgy time.

It was around then that he began suffering from abdominal pains.

He went to Paris where he fell for a ballet choreographer who chose his boy-for-the-night by lining up lads [mostly his dancers] in a row and measuring their dicks hard. Valentino took part and won for that night. One boy called his endowment Herculean.

His doctors were certain they could successfully operate and cure his abdominal stress. They couldn't. At 31 he was dead, the end of a near-perfect life.

Ramón Novarro

Ramón Novarro had his own villa at the Garden of Allah, located next to that of director Ernst Lubitsch, William Power and Carol Lombard. Unknown today, Novarro was an immense star, whose film *Ben Hur* was number one in the box office before being dethroned by *Gone with the Wind.*

In the times of Ramón Novarro and Valentino homosexuality was considered anything from a psychological disorder to a form of sexual perversion, and during Anthony Perkins's years doctors claimed it could be cured. Perkins underwent treatment to change him into a heterosexual, eventually marrying and producing children. To escape being found out Tyrone Power married. Novarro always congratulated himself for having escaped the tender trap, while others, like Tyrone Power, had to take part in orgies where the naked boys, fucking their girls, their hard asses rising and falling, gave Power the hard-on he needed to perform with his wife.

Tired of Valentino's prima donna demands, directors sought a replacement, and Novarro got his chance. He was born in Mexico near enough to the American border to pick up English, and in 1916, at the age of 17, he went to California to live with family members, passing through customs where he was given a physical examination and deloused. In Los Angeles he tried to find bit-parts in films, while earning money by posing nude in art classes and ushering in theaters.

Ramón got a role in a dancing scene in Valentino's *The Four Horsemen of the Apocalypse*, in 1921, a film that cost a whopping $608,000 in a time when a film's budget was $60,000, but turned out to be a success only second to Griffith's *The Birth of a Nation* (1915), bringing in $14 million, saving Metro from bankruptcy and making Valentino a star overnight. Rex Ingram directed the film and sickened by Valentino's ever-increasing demands, said he could replace the mercurial actor with anyone he chose. Valentino left for Famous Players and Ingram signed on Novarro, determined to unseat Valentino. Novarro's career was helped along also thanks to Valentino's continued salary disputes with his new studio [*and* the strong possibility that Novarro was Ingram's lover, eased by the fact that they were only six years apart in age]. Ingram starred Novarro in MGM's *The Arab*, which proved a success although Ingram, who hated and was hated by MGM's director Mayer, suffered from depression. Novarro soon had a new house with all the accoutrements of wealth, a swimming pool and sauna.

Goldwyn studios bought the rights to *Ben Hur* for an unheard-of $1 million. Valentino was chosen for the principle role but still embroiled in salary disputes, the role went to Novarro, chosen over John Gilbert, considered a drunk. Homophobe, Mayer apparently knew nothing of Novarro's homosexuality. At a cost of $4 million, the 1925 film would have to rake in $11 million to breakeven, making it the most expensive film until *Gone with the Wind* 14 years later. It eventually earned only $9.4 million.

Garbo and Novarro.

In the looks category, John Gilbert had a stronger virility that made him more acceptable to male audiences, while Valentino's ''eye rolling and nostril flaring'' as André Soares puts it in his excellent *Beyond Paradise, The Life of Ramón Novarro*, was too androgynous, and Novarro too pretty, for male appreciation. Herbert Howe, Novarro's lover during this time, was a publicist who set out to prove, in print, that his bed partner was a rampant heterosexual.

Howe and Novarro

When Howe and Novarro broke up Howe wrote that Novarro had once said, ''I have so little to give,'' which had exactly been the case, according to Howe [referring perhaps to Novarro's talent, perhaps to his virile member, or perhaps to both].

Seven years after his first film, he spoke, as sound came to pictures, and his voice was deemed perfect. He starred in *Mata Hari* with Garbo but little by little male stars like Gable and James Cagney were favored, and due to his declining looks Novarro turned to alcohol, appearing at a party entirely naked. But he remained a huge star in Europe and was assailed by fans when he toured Latin America.

Where guys had begged to be in his company, now he went to rent boys, one of whom, identified only as Chuck, procured dozens of his buddies for the aging Novarro. He would never be involved in a sex scandal, although his drinking led to numerous automobile accidents.

Scotty Bowers knew Novarro when he was in his fifties. Because he was often drunk, he was often impotent, and the cure for it was drinking the semen of young men. ''So I would bring five or six young guys over to his house", wrote Bowers in his book *Full Service* [see Sources], "and Ramón would call one at a time into his bedroom to suck them off."

Then he received a phone call from someone who would service him for money. Novarro got a description of the boy's physical attributes and invited him and his brother over to his home. The boys stripped to their briefs and one went into Novarro's bedroom where he beat Novarro, trying to find out where he hid his cash. His brother came in and while he took over the beating, the other brother, in bloodstained shorts, paraded in front of a mirror in one of Novarro's hats, twirling one of his canes. The brothers, 17 and 22, left the house with $20. The autopsy claimed Novarro had died of asphyxiation, the brothers said he had choked on his own blood--but Scotty Bowers insists he had been suffocated by a dildo that Valentino had given him years before, an exact replica of Valentino's 10-inch cock.

One of the brothers committed suicide, the other was jailed, and Ramón Novarro's star was added to Hollywood's Walk of Fame.

Bonnie and Clyde

Roaring Twenties' crimes of another nature were propagated by Bonnie Parker and Clyde Barrow, Clyde born in Texas in 1909 to a close-knit family whose parents were too occupied making a living to control their eight children. Early on Clyde and his brother Buck, apparently influenced by films showing the exploits of Jesse James and Cole Younger, took to robbing grocery stores and gas stations, adding the robbery of banks and eventually murder in reprisal for beatings they'd received by prison guards, revenge that would cost a total of nine lawmen their lives, as well as four others, often caught in crossfires.

Clyde had been convicted of auto theft at an early age and in prison he killed an inmate with a lead pipe when sexually assaulted, but a friend serving a life term took the blame. To get out of prison early, Clyde chopped off two toes, which left him with a limp for the rest of his life. His family noted that imprisonment changed him ''from a school boy into a rattle snake.''

Clyde, 20, hooked up with Bonnie Parker, 19, introduced to him by a mutual friend, and with Buck and Buck's wife Blanche they formed the core of the gang, later joined by W.D. Jones, 16, a boyhood friend of the family whom Clive, seven years older, called ''boy''. The day after joining the gang Jones and Clyde killed Doyle Johnson when Johnson reached for Clyde's throat through the window of the car Clyde was stealing. Clyde warning him he would shoot, and when Johnson kept on throttling him, he did. Five days later both killed Deputy Sheriff Malcolm Davis who had been sent to arrest them for the killing of Johnson.

Clyde and Bonnie, Jones, Methvin and the bullet-riddled car.

The couple was immortalized in Arthur Penn's 1967 masterpiece *Bonnie and Clyde*, the beauty of Warren Beatty equaled only by Peter O'Toole's in *Lawrence of Arabia.*

Bonnie had married at age 15, and although soon separated from her thieving husband [but not divorced], she was wearing his ring when she died. From his prison cell her husband stated that her death was better that way, "much better than being caught."

Blanche became a friend of Warren Beatty. She hated her portrayal as a screaming bitch in the film, a role that won the woman who played her, Estelle Parsons, the film's only Oscar for acting. Beatty produced it at the cost of $2.5 million, and it immediately raked in $70 million, making Beatty a multi-millionaire.

The times were so difficult and foreclosures so common that the public in general was willing to forgive the gang when they robbed banks, run by the wealthy. Clyde would tell those trapped in the banks to pocket their money, and he was in the habit of capturing law enforcement officers, taking them on long rides before releasing them with enough cash to see them home. But when forced to fight for their lives, he and his men were pitiless. Despite a treasury of thousands of dollars [hundreds of thousands in today's money], they were forced to camp out or hold up in dumps that served as motels, where their secretive attitude, loud fights when drunk, and their way of paying in freshly-minted silver dollars for the food they bought, aroused suspicion. The result was endless firefights with the police who had been alerted to their presence, one shootout that took Buck's life and blinded Blanche in one eye for life. Clyde and Bonnie were wounded on several occasions, and during a driving accident Bonnie was severely burned. As for Jones, he had been so riddled that when he tried to join the army, after serving his time in jail, he was turned down because during his physical examination a bullet and buckshot were disclosed by X-rays. Said Jones later, ''I got shot in the side at Joplin, and my belly ached so bad I thought the bullet had stopped there. Clyde wrapped an elm branch with gauze and pushed it through the hole in my side and out my back. The bullet had gone clean through me so we knew it would heal.''

While searching one of the gang's hideouts, the police came across film showing Bonnet clenching a cigar, and her poems, all published in the nearby town's *Globe*, making them instant celebrities when picked up nationwide in other papers.

For the police, the straw that broke the camel's back was when Clyde dared attack the Texas Department of Corrections to free incarcerated gang members, during which a guard, Joe Crowson, was killed. Promising to avenge his death, the Department hired legendary Texas Ranger Captain Frank Hamer-- a god to other rangers and policemen--to bring Clyde and his gang to justice. Hamer was officially credited with 53 kills and himself had suffered 17 wounds.

For the public, the last straw was when the gang kidnapped two young highway patrolmen that they shot to death [under circumstances that have never been elucidated, some stating at Bonnie gave the *coup de grâce*, others that it was a third gang member, Henry Methvin, who executed the two lads.]. Five days later they shot another policeman, William Campbell, soon followed by an additional three killings.

It is little wonder that Hamer and his posse of five gave them no warning as they drove into an ambush at 9:00 in the morning on May 23, 1934. The car was hit by 130 bullets, then by shotgun fire when the rifles were empty, followed by hand pistols when they'd run out of shotgun cartridges.

In 1933 Bonnie and Clyde had kidnapped an undertaker who'd come upon them stealing his car. Bonnie purportedly laughed when he disclosed his profession, joking that perhaps one day they'd need him to work on them. The man, Dillard Darby, was called in to assist at their embalming.

Clyde chose the epitaph on the stone placed over the grave he shared with his brothers: Gone but not forgotten.

Jones was arrested and during his confession he related the gang's sex lives. He was sentenced to 15 years, lenient because he had come clean. He was later killed by a woman's boyfriend when he came to her aid, the boyfriend having misunderstood Jones's intentions.

Frank Hamer made headlines again when he tried to help Coke Stevenson in his challenge to Lyndon Johnson during an election for the Senate, related in Robert Caro's life of Lyndon Johnson, the greatest biography of our times, an absolute must-read, in several volumes.

Beatty's portrayal of Clyde's sexuality was letter-perfect. Clyde may have been bisexual, but perhaps not enough to have concluded with Bonnie, although after avoiding her throughout the whole film, they do, in producer Beatty's version, sleep together, Beatty's Clyde appearing entirely cocky the next morning. Clyde's years in prison certainly encouraged his homosexual bent, and it is known that he and Jones disappeared for an entire month together in 1933. Said Jones in an interview: ''I've heard stories since that Clyde was homosexual, or, as they say in the pen, a ''punk'', but they ain't true. Maybe it was Clyde's quiet, polite manner and his slight build that fooled folks."

In Arthur Penn's film *Bonnie and Clyde*, Penn invents a character, C.W. Moss, who is a composite of W.D. Jones and Henry Methvin, a handsome lad that Clyde freed from the Texas Department of Corrections, a boy often cited as another of Clyde's lovers. Methvin is also often cited as the murderer of the two young policemen, but, as said, the circumstances of their executions are unclear.

It was Methvin's father who contacted Hamer, disclosing the whereabouts of Bonnie and Clyde in exchange for Hamer's promise that his son would not be given the death penalty. Paroled in 1942, Methvin, aged 36, was hit by a train when, drunk, he fell while crossing a railroad track.

JC

The creator of this marvel was Joseph Christian Leyendecker, called JC, 1874-1951, the inventor of modern magazine design, producing over 400 covers. Born in Germany, his family emigrated to Chicago when JC was 8. He studied in Paris with his brother where they were influenced by the work of Toulouse Lautrec. Both returned to Chicago when JC was 25 where he was commissioned to illustrate men's wear, often suits and Arrow shirts, using as a model his 17-year-old lover Charles Beach, JC 29 at the time. During W.W.I he did recruitment posters and created the Kellogg Kids for Kellogg's Corn Flakes. He and his lover moved to New Rochelle, New York, where they hosted extravagant parties attended by celebrities and the social aristocracy. His decline came with the Wall Street Crash of 1929, after which he retired with Beach until his heart attack at his New Rochelle estate in 1951.

The homoerotic beauty of his models, a combination of jock and dandy, wrote one admirer, is said to have elicited more fan mail from men than did Valentino himself. His brother Frank, as homosexual as JC, died at an early age from drug abuse.

SOURCES

(1) From *Wikipedia*.
(2) See my book *Buckingham*.
(3) See my book *Omnisexuality*.
(4) See my book *Boarding School Homosexuality*.
(5) See my X-rated book *Hustlers*.
(6) See my book *Rent Boys*.

(7) See my book *Sailors and Homosexuality*.
(8) See my book *Renaissance Homosexuality*.
(9) See my book *Phallus*.
(10) See my book *Christ Has His John, I Have My George*: *The History of British Homosexuality*.
(11) See my book *Venice*.
(12) See my book *Capris, Homosexual Paradise*.
(13) See my book *All-Male Pornography*.
(14) See my book *French Homosexuality*.
(15) See my book *Tasmania*.
(16) See my book *The Bloomsbury Set*.
(17) See my book *German Homosexuality*.
(18) See my book *Sparta*.
(19) See my book *The Sacred Band*.
(20) See my book *The World's Greatest All-Male Film Directors*.
(21) See my book *Homosexual Secret Societies*.
(22) See my book *The Garden of Allah*.
(23) See my book *American Homosexual Giants*.
(24) See my book *TROY*.
(25) See book *Alexander and Hephaestion*.
(26) See my book *Exploration Giants*.
(27) See my book *Hollywood's Homosexual History*.
(28) See my book *Male Self-Pleasuring*.
(29) See my book *Hadrian and Antinous*.
(30) See my book *Cellini*.
(31) See my book *Greek Homosexuality*.
(32) Darwin Porter and Danforth Prince's *James Dean*.
(33) See my book *The History of Orgies*.
(34) See my book *Elagabalus*.
(35) See my book *Roman Homosexuality*.

Aggleton, Peter, *Men Who Sell Sex*, 1999.
Aldrich, Robert, *The Seduction of the Mediterranean*, 1993.
Aldrich and Wotherspoon, *Who's Who in Gay and Lesbian History*, 2001.
Ankerich, Michael, *The Sound of Silence*, 1998.
Baatz, Simon, *For the Thrill of It*, 2008.
Beachy, Robert, *Gay Berlin*, 2014. Marvelous.
Bellori, *Caravaggio*, circa 1600.
Bentley, Jim, *Last Time I drew A Crowd*, 2005.
Bicheno, Hugh, *Vendetta*, 2007.
Boswell, John, *Christianity, Social Tolerance, and Homosexuality*, 1980.
Boswell, John, *Same-Sex Unions*, 1994.
Bowers, Scotty, *Full Service*, 2012.

Full Service is a wonderful book by Scotty Bowers, a 150-hour interview taped and put in book form by Lionel Frieberg. It's a miracle because Bowers decided to tape his tell-all in 2012 when Scotty was 88. Bowers opened a gas station and because he was a good-looking ex-Marine, always willing to turn an extra buck in the American tradition, he offered himself for rent, and as his clientele increased he hired Marine friends to care for the needs of Hollywood actors, producers, *et al.*, Marines who serviced guys and/or gals, and later women to service guys and other women, among whom was Katherine Hepburn.

His Marines often had a great time, were served great food around great pools, and did what his clients wanted, which was often just a human presence and a little mutual jerking off. Some of the boys wound up living with the men, as found in the scene from *Some Like It Hot* where Jack Lemmon returns from his date with Osgood and declares to Tony Curtis that he and Osgood were going to get married. "Why would a guy marry another guy?" asked Curtis. "For *security!*" exclaims Lemmon. Numerous Scotty-Bower Full-Service assignations took place in the Garden of Allah.

Bowers and his Marines were easy-going guys, and having fun with them must have been fun in itself. In the following pages the reader will get to know Scotty, who I hope has at the very least another 88 years ahead of him.

Bramly, Serge, *Leonardo*, 1988.
Bret, David, *Clark Gable*, 2007.
Bret, David, *Errol Flynn, Gentleman Hellraiser*, 2004,
Bret, David, *Valentino*, 1998.
Bret, David, *Trailblazers*, 2009.
Bull, Lew, *Memoirs of a Hustler*, 2010.
Burg, B.R., *Gay Warriors*, 2002.
Calimach, Andrew, *Lover's Legends*, 2002.
Callow, Simon, *Charles Laughton*, 1995.
Capote, A Reader, Abacus, 1989.
Carpenter, Edward, *The Intermediate Sex*, 1912.
Carson, H.A., *a thousand and one night stands*, 2001.
Cavel Benjamin, *Rumble, Young Man, Rumble*, 2003.
Charyn, Jerome, *Movieland: Hollywood and the Great American Dream Culture*, 1989.
Clark, Adrian and Jeremy Dronfield, *Queer Saint, Peter Watson*, 2015.
Clark, Gerald, *Capote*, 1988.
Cowan, Thomas, *Gay Men and Women Who Enriched*

the World, 1988/
Crompton, Louis, *Byron and Greek Love*, 1985.
Crompton, Louis, *Homosexuality and Civilization*, 2003.
Defored, Frank, *Big Bill Tilden*, 1975.
Davidson, James, *Courtesans and Fishcakes*, 1998.
Davidson, James, *The Greeks and Greek Love*, 2007.
Davidson, Michael, *The World, The Flesh and Myself*, 1977.
Dorais, Michel, *Rent Boys*, 2002,
Eisler, Benita, *BYRON Child of Passion, Fool of Fame*, 2000. Wonderful.
Ellmann, Richard, *Oscar Wilde*, 1987.
Escoffier, Jeffrey, *Bigger Than Life*, 2009.
Evans, Robert, *The Kid Stays in the Picture*, 1994.
Fiore, Carlo, *The Brando I Knew*, 1974.
Gilmore, John, *Laid Bare*, 1997.
Gilmore, John, *Live Fast—Die Young*, 1997.
Graham, Sheilah, *Garden of Allah*, 1969
Halperin David M. *One Hundred Years of Homosexuality*, 1990.
Harris, Frank, *My Life and Loves*, 1925.
Hibbard, Allen, *Paul Bowles*, 1993.
Hine, Daryl, *Puerilities*, 2001.
Hofler, Robert, *Party Animals,* 2010.
Hofler, Robert, *The Man Who Invented Rock Hudson*, 2005.
Hogan, Steve, *Completely Queer, Gay and Lesbian Encyclopedi*a, 1998.
Holland Tom, *Rubicon*, 2003.
Hughes-Hallett, *Heroes*, 2004.
Hutchinson, Robert, *House of Treason*, 2009.
Isherwood, Christopher, *Christopher and His Kind*, 1976.

Isherwood, Christopher, *Diaries*, vol. one, 2011.
Jeffers, H. Paul, Sal Mineo, *His Life, Murder and Mystery*, 2000.
Kanfer, Stefan, *Marlon Brando*, 2008.
Katz, Jonathan Ned, *Love Stories*, 2001.
Kearns, Michael, *The Truth is Bad Enough*, 2012,
Kelly, Ian, *Casanova: Actor Lover Priest Spy*, 2008.
Korda, Michael, *HERO The Life and Legend of Lawrence of Arabia*, 2010.
Lahr, John, *Prick Up Your Ears, The Biography of Joe Orton*, 1978
Lahr, John, *Tennessee Williams, Mad Pilgrimage of the Flesh*, 2014.
Lyons, Mathew, *The Favourite*, 2011.
Macintyre, Ben, *The Man Who Would Be King*, 2004.
McDougal, Dennis, *Privileged Son*, 2001.
Mackay, John Henry, *The Hustler*, 2002.
Manchester, William, *A World Lit Only By Fire*, 1993.
Mann, William, *Wisecracker*, 1998.
Mann, William, *Men Who Love Men*, 2007.
Mann, William, *The Men from the Boys*, 1998.
Manso, Peter, *Brando*, 1994.
McBrien, William, *Cole Porter*, 2000.
McCann, Graham, *Rebel Males*, 1991.
McGilligan, Patrick, *A Double Life--George Cukor*, 1991.
McNamara, Robert P., *The Times Square Hustler*, 1994.
Merritt, Rich, *Secrets of a Gay Marine Porn Star*, 2005.
Minichiello, Victor and John Scott, *Male Sex Work and Society*, 2014.
Money, James, *Capri, Island of Pleasure*, 1986.
Nicholl, Charles, *The Reckoning*, 2002.
Niven, David, *Bring on the Empty Horses*, 1975.

Niven, David, *The Moon's a Balloon*, 1971.
Norton, Rictor, *My Dear Boy, Gay Love Letters*, 1998.
O'Hara, Scott, *Autopornography, A Memoir of Life in the Lust Lane*, 1997.
Oosterhuis, Harry, *Homosexuality and Male Bonding*, 1991.
Ostrow, Steve, *Live at the Continental*, 2007.
Paring, Justin, *The life and times of Samuel Steward*, 2010.
Parini, Jay, *Empire of Self, A Life of Gore Vidal*, 2015.
Parish, James Robert, *The Hollywood Book of Death*, 2002.
Parker, Peter, *Isherwood A Life*, 2004,
Pearce, Joseph, *The Unmasking of Oscar Wilde*, 2000.
Plimpton, George, *Truman Capote*, 1998.
Plutarch's Lives, Modern Library.
Porter, Darwin & Roy Moseley, *Damn You, Scarlett O'Hara*, 2011.
Porter, Darwin and Danforth Prince, *Pink Triangle*, 2014.
Porter, Darwin and Danforth Prince, *James Dean*, 2016.
Porter, Darwin, *Brando Unzipped*, 2004.
Porter, Darwin, *Howard Hughes*, 2010.
Porter, Darwin, *Paul Newman*, 2009.
Rader, Dotson, *Blood Dues*, 1974.
Reed, Jeremy, *The Dilly*, 2014.
Reid, B.L., *The Lives of Roger Casement*, 1976.
Robb, Peter, *Street Fight in Naples*, 2010.
Roen, Paul, *High Camp*, 1994.
Rocke, Michael, *Forbidden Friendships*, 1996. Fabulous/indispensible.
Rolfe, Frederick, Letters to Charles Kains Jackson, *My*

Dear KJ..., 2015.
Russo, William/Jan Merlin, *MGM Makes Boys Town*, 2012.
Sawyer-Lauçanno, *An Invisible Specter, Paul Bowles*, 1989.
Scurr, Ruth, *Fatal Purity*, 2007.
Setz, Wolfram, *The Sins of the Cities of the Plain*, 1881.
Seymour, Craig, *All I could Bare*, 2008.
Shakespeare, Nicholas, *Bruce Chatwin*, 1999.
Shaw, Aiden, *Sordid Truths*, 2009.
Shelden, Michael, *Graham Greene, The Man Within*, 1994.
Sheridan, Alan, *André Gide*, 1998.
Shilts, Randy, *And the Band Played on*, 1987.
Skidmore, Chris, *Death and the Virgin*, 2010.
Soares, André, *The Life of Ramon Novarro*, 2010.
Spoto, Donald, *The Kindness of Strangers*, 1997.
Spoto, Donald, *The Life of Tennessee Williams*, 1985.
Teeman, Tim, *In Bed with Gore Vidal*, 2013.
Vanderbilt, Arthur, *Best-Kept Boy in the World*, 2014.
Vernant, Jean-Pierre, *Mortals and Immortals*, 1991.
Vidal, Gore, *Palimpsest: A Memoir*, 1995.
Virgil, *The Aeneid*, Everyman's Library, Knopf, 1907.
Walsh, Kenneth M., *wasn't tomorrow wonderful?* 2014.
Watson, Steven, *Factory Made*, 2003.
Wikipedia: Research today is impossible without the aid of this monument.
Wilson, Derek, *The Uncrowned Kings of England*, 2005.
Winecoff, Charles, *Anthony Perkins, split image*, 1996.
Wolff, Geoffrey, *Black Sun: The Violent Eclipse of Harry Crosby*, 1976.
Zeeland, Steven, *Sailors and Sexual Identity*, 1995.
Vidal, Gore, *Palimpsest*, 1995.

Woods, Gregory, *Homintern*, 2016.
Wright, Ed, *History's Greatest Scandals*, 2006.

INDEX

Please note that the page numbers are *passim*. An example, Gide 76 – 102, means that Gide is found within these pages, but not necessarily on *every* page.

Adelswärd-Fersen, Alex 158-167
Adelswärd-Fersen, Jacques de' 158-167
Adelswärd-Fersen, Renold 158-167
Aigle à deux têtes, L' 114-140
Akademos 158-167
Alexander the Great 38-43
Allégret, Marc 114-140, 140-153
Antinous 97-99
Apostles, Society of 23-35
Après-midi d'un faune, L' 114-140
Arab, The 195-199
Arlen, Richard 183-185
Around the World in 80 Days 114-140
Au temps de boeuf sur le toit 114-140
Auden, W.H. 63-73, 78-82
Aumont, Jean-Pierre 101-114
Ayala, Serge 114-140
Bacon, Francis 23-35
Baird, John 6-23
baiser de Narcisse, Le 158-167
Baker, Josephine 101-114
Bal des Quat'z'Arts 101-114
Barnum and Bailey Circus 153-158
Barrow, Buck 199-205

Barrow, Clyde 199-205
Barthelmess, Richard 189-195
Beach, Charles 205
Beaton, Cecil 57-61
Beatty, Warren 199-205
Béjart, Maurice 153-158
Belle et la Bête, La 114-140
Ben Hur 195-199
Bennett, James Gordon 177-180
Benson, Arthur 23-35
Benson, Edward 50-55
Bergman, Ingrid 114-140
Bernhardt, Sarah 114-140
Beverly Hills Hotel 167-175
Bezos, Jeff 6-23
Birth of a Nation, The 195-199
Blood and Sand 185-189, 189-195
Bloomsbury Set 6-23, 23-35
Blüher, Hans 97-99
Boeuf sur le Toit 6-23
Bolero 153-158
Bonjean, Jacques 114-140
Bouly, Léon 101-114
Bourgoint, Jean 114-140
Bourgoint, Jeanne 114-140
Bovy, Berthe 114-140
Bowers, Scotty 195-199
Boy with Rabbit 85
Brand 97-99
Brand, Adolf 63-73, 86-89
Brandford, Edwin 38-43
Breker, Arno 100, 114-140
Brinkley, John 177-180

Brooks, John 50-55
Brown, Al 114-140
Buckingham 23-35
Cabaret 63-73
Cahiers d'André Walter, Les 140-153
Cambridge 23-35
Campbell, William 199-205
Can-Can 101-114
Canard enchaîné 114-140
Capone, Al 6-23
Carné, Marcel 101-114
Caro, Robert 199-205
Carpenter, Edward 43-50
Carter, Howard 6-23
Castorp, Hans 94-97
Chaeronea, Order of 38-43
Chandler, Harry 177-180
Chanel, Coco 6-23, 114-140
Charles II 23-35
Chevalier, Maurice 101-114
Christie, Agatha 6-23
Churchill, Winston 55-57
Cleveland Street Telegram Scandal 35-38
Cocteau, Jean 101-114, 114-140, 140-153
Cohen, Mickey 185-189
Colette 101-114
Comstock Laws 6-23
Concerto pour la main gauche 153-158
Confessions of Felix Krull, The 94-97
Conrad, Joseph 61-63
Cooke, Tim 78-82
Corvo, Baron 50-55
Corydon 140-153

Cottam, Samuel 38-43
Counterfeiters, The 140-153
Coward, Noël 57-61
Crane, Walter 101-114
Cranmar, Thomas 23-35
Crawford, Joan 167-175
Cromwell, Oliver 23-35
Crowson, Joe 199-205
Cukor, George 6-23, 167-175
Curie, Marie 101-114
Cyrano de Bergerac 114-140
Daphnis et Chloé 153-158
Darby, Dillard 199-205
Dargelos, Pierre 114-140
Darwin, Charles 23-35
Daudet, Alphonse 114-140
Daudet, Lucien 114-140
Daven, André 189-195
Davies, Marion 177-180
Davis, Malcolm 199-205
Dawaere, Patrick 140-153
Dean, James 6-23
Der Eigene 86-89, 97-99
Dermit, Édouard 114-140
Desbordes, Jean 114-140
Diable au corps, Le 114-140
Diaghilev, Serge 153-158
Disney, Walt 6-23
Doheny, Edward 176
Doheny, Ned 176
Douglas, George Norman 61-63
Dr. No 57-61
Drawings of a Sleeper 114-140

Dreyfus Affaire 101-114
Drôle de Drame 101-114
E.M. Forster 43-50
Edward, Prince of Wales 55-57
Ehrenberg, Paul 94-97
Eisenhower, Dwight 6-23
Eisenstein, Sergei 78-82
Enfants terribles, Les 114-140
Entwistle, Lillian 167-175
Escoffier, Auguste 101-114
Exposition Universelle 101-114
Fairbanks Jr., Douglas 167-175
Fairbanks, Douglas 167-175, 183-185
Fall, Albert 176
Fiers, robert de 114-140
Flapper 6-23
Flemings, Alexander 6-23
Flynn, Errol 185-189
Folies Bergère 101-114
Forbes, Vivian 85
Four Horsemen of the Apocalypse, The 189-199
Fouts, Denham 114-140
Franks, Bobby 180-183
Frederick the Great 63-73
Fresnay, Pierre 114-140
Freud, Sigmund 73-78
Freundschaft, Die 91-92
Friedländer, Paul 86-89
Full Service 195-199
Gable, Clark 167-175
Gallais, Alphonse 158-167
Gallé, Émile 101-114
Garbo 6-23, 195-199

Gard, Martin du 140-153
Garden of Allah 185-189
Gerber, Henry 6-23, 93
Gershwin, George 153-158
Gesmar, Charles 101-114
Gide, André 78-82, 114-140, 140-153
Gide, Madeleine 140-153
Giese, Karl 78-82
Gilbert, John 6-23, 195-199
Gilbert, Yvette 101-114
Gloeden, Wilhelm von 89-91
God That Failed, The 140-153
Goddard, Robert 6-23
Gone with the Wind 195-199
Goulue, La 101-114
Grant, Cary 177-180
Grant, Duncan 23-35
Great Depression 6-23
Green, Burton 167-175
Greene, Graham 61-63
Greystone Mansion 176
Griffith 195-199
Griffith J. Griffith
Griffith Park 175
Griffith, D.W. 167-175, 195-199
Grynszpan, Harschel 114-140
Guitry, Sasha 114-140
Gymnasium 82-84
Gymnopédies 153-158
Hadrian, Emperor 97-99
Hailsham, Lord 6-23
Haines, William 167-175, 177-180
Hamer, Frank 199-205

Hammond, Charles 35-38
Harvard, John 23-35
Haussman, George-Eugène 101-114
Haxton, Gerald 50-55
Hayfever 57-61
Hearst, William Randolph 177-180
Hébertot, Jacques 189-195
Henry II 23-35
Henry III 23-35
Henry VIII 23-35
Herald 177-180
Heuser, Klaus 94-97
Higher Sodomy 23-35
Hill, Virginia 185-189
Hirschfeld, Magnus 78-82
Hitler 100
Hollywood Hotel 167-175
Honegger, Arthur 153-158
Howe, Herbert 195-199
Hurd, E.C. 167-175
Hymnaire d'Adonis, L' 158-167
Im Schwimmbad 8
Inconcevable Jean Cocteau, L' 114-140
Intermediate Sex 43-50
IRA 55-57
Isherwood, Christopher 63-73
Israel, Hermann
Ives, George Cecil 38-43
J'adore 114-140
Jackson, Kains 38-43
Jahn, Hellmuth 82-84
James I/VI 23-35
James, Jesse 199-205

Jansen, Wilhelm 99
Jauregg, Julius Wagner von 73-78
Johns, W.D. 199-205
Johnson, Doyle 199-205
Johnson, Lyndon 199-205
Kerouac, Jack 73-78
Keynes, Maynard 6-23, 38-43
Khill, Marcel 114-140
Kiss of Narcissus, The 158-167
Krupp, Frederick von 63-73, 89-91
Laliques, René 101-114
Last Picture Show, The 6-23
Lawrence, D.H. 6-23
Leopold, Nathan 180-183
Leyendecker, Joseph 6-23
Leyendecker, Joseph Christian 205
Liebermann, Max 85
Life Plus 99 Years 180-183
Lindbergh, Charles 6-23
Lindsell, John 50-55
Livre blanc 114-140
Loeb, Richard 180-183
Lolita 57-61
Lord Lillian 158-167
Lorrain, Jean 114-140
Lower Sodomy 23-35
Lunel, Maurice Tranchant de 114-140
Mackay, John Henry 84
Mackenzie, Compton 61-63
Magic Mountain 94-97
Magnani, Anna 114-140
Magnus Hirschfeld 73-78
Maillol, Aristide 100

Mallarmé, Stéphane 153-158
Mallory, George 23-35
Mann, Klaus 63-73
Mann, Thomas 94-97
Männer 91-92
Marais, Jean 114-140, 140-153
Marks and Spencer 6-23
Marshall Plan 6-23
Martens, Armin 94-97
Mary, Queen of England 23-35
Massine, Léonide 114-140
Massot, Pierre de 114-140
Mata Hari 195-199
Mather, Ernest 38-43
Maugham, Somerset 50-55
Maurice 43-50
Max, Édouard de 114-140
Mayer, L.B. 167-175
McCormick, Harold 177-180
McMurtry, Larry 6-23
Meerscheidt-Hüllessem 78-82
Melling, Alec 38-43
Melville, Herman 43-50
Mémoires du Baron Jacques, Les 158-167
Merrill, George 43-50
Methvin, Henry 199-205
Michelangelo 100
Michelin, Édouard 101-114
Mickey Mouse 6-23
Miede, Max 86-89
Mistinguett 101-114
Moon and Sixpence 50-55
Moro, Il 89-91

Moulin Rouge 6-23, 101-114
Moulin, Jean 114-140
Mount Rushmore 6-23
Mountbatten, Lord 55-57
Mussolini, Benito 6-23
Mussorgsky 153-158
Nameless Love 84
Nazimova, Alla 167-175, 185-189, 189-195
Newton Arthur 35-38
Newton, Isaac 23-35
Nicholson, John Gambril 38-43
Niemann, Albert 63-73
Nietzsche 180-183
Nijinsky 114-140
Noailles, Anna de 114-140
Noces, Les 153-158
Novarro, Ramón 195-199
O'Toole, Peter 199-205
Oedipe Roi 114-140
Orenstein, Arbie 153-158
Orphée 114-140
Oxbridge 23-35
Oxford 23-35
Parade 114-140
Parker, Al 6-23
Parker, Bonnie 199-205
Parker, Dorothy 185-189
Passage to India, A 43-50
Passe Muraille, La 114-140
Payne, Graham 57-61
Penn, Arthur 199-205
Persifal 97-99
Philip of Macedonia 38-43

Philipe, Gérard 140-153, 189-195
Philips, Harry 50-55
Philpot, Glyn 85
Pickford 183-185
Pickford, Mary 167-175
Picture of Dorian Gray, The 140-153
Pictures at an Exhibition 153-158
Plato 43-50
Plunkett, Hugh 176
Plüschow, Guglielmo 89-91
Porte étroite, La 140-153
Portrait of Miriam Green, The 158-167
Poulenc, Francis 153-158
Power, Tyrone 185-189
Prep Schools and Universities 23-35
Proust 101-114
Queen Christina 6-23
Radiguet, Raymond 114-140
Radszuweit, Friedrich 91-92
Radszuweit, Martin-Butzko 91-92
Raft, George 185-189
Rambova, Natcha 189-195
Rath, Ernst von 114-140
Ravel, Maurice 153-158
Reich, George 114-140
Reich, William 73-78
Renard, Jules 114-140
Rimsky-Korsakov 153-158
Rogers, Buddy 183-185
Röhm, Ernst 63-73
Room with a View, A 43-50
Rorem, Ned 57-61
Rostand, Maurice 114-140

Ruth, Babe 6-23
Sachs, Maurice 114-140
Sacre du printemps 114-140, 153-158
Sacred Band 38-43, 97-99
Saint-Saëns, Camille 153-158
Sainte 153-158
Salinger, J.D. 73-78
San Simeon Castle 177-180
Satie, Erik 153-158
Schneider, Sascha 82-84
Scopes Monkey Trial 6-23
Scott, Randolph 177-180
Searle, Alan 50-55
Sears Roebuck 6-23
Sessums, Kevin 183-185
Seventeen 177-180
Shéhérazade 153-158
Sheik, The 189-195
Shields, Jimmy 167-175
Siegel, Bugsy 185-189
Snyder, Louis 63-73
So Sang Marsyas 158-167 158-167
Society for Human Rights 6-23, 93
Sodom and Gomorrah 114-140
Somerset, Arthur 35-38
Speer, Albert 100
Spender, Stephen 114-140
St. Sebastian 85
Stalin 55-57, 100
Stanley, Henry 177-180
Stanwyck, Barbara 185-189
Stepanoff, Daniel 82-84
Stevenson, Coke 199-205

Stravinsky 6-23, 153-158
Streatfeild, Philip 57-61
Student Revolt of 1969 73-78
Summers, Montague 38-43
Swanson, Gloria 167-175
Symonds, John 23-35
Symposium 43-50
Thackeray, Makepeace 23-35
Thatcher, Margaret 23-35
There Will Be Blood 176
Tilden, William 167-175
tombeau de Couperin, Le 153-158
Tonio Kröger 94-97
Toulouse-Lautrec 101-114
Train bleu, le 101-114
Tuchs, Thomas 63-73
Tuke, Scott 38-43
Tutankhamun 6-23
Ungewitters, Richard 97-99
Valentino, Rudolph 189-199
Vampire, His Kith and Kin, The 38-43
Verne, Jules 114-140
Victor, Albert 35-38
Vidal, Gore 55-57, 140-153
Vignola, Robert 177-180
Villa Jovis 158-167
Viñes, Ricardo 153-158
Voix humaine, La 114-140
Voltaire 63-73
Wagner, Richard 97-99
Wandervogel Movement 97-99
Warren, Hans de 158-167
Weber, Louise 101-114

Weimar Republic 63-73
Werewolf, The 38-43
When Knighthood Was in Flower 177-180
When Love Grows Cold 189-195
Where Angels Fear to Tread 43-50
Whirlwind of Death 153-158
Whitley, H.J. 167-175
Whitman, Walt 97-99
Wibbels, Henry 114-140
Wilde 140-153
Wilde, Oscar 23-35, 38-43
Wilson, Harold 55-57
Wilson, Jack 57-61
Wings 183-185
Wisecracker 167-175
Wittgenstein, Paul 153-158
Władysław, Moes 94-97
Young Rajah 189-195
Younger, Cole 199-205
Youth 158-167
Youth in a Blue Coat 82-84
Zola, Émile 101-114

[My autobiography: *Michael Hone His World, His Loves*]

Made in United States
North Haven, CT
25 July 2022

21778905R00126